HOGAN
ON THE GREEN

Also by John Andrisani:

HOGAN
ON THE GREEN

A Detailed Analysis of the Revolutionary Putting Method of Golf Legend **BEN HOGAN**

JOHN ANDRISANI

RODALE

Rodale books may be purchased for business or promotional use or for special sales. For information, please write to: Special Markets Department, Rodale Inc., 733 Third Avenue, New York, NY 10017

Printed in the United States of America

Rodale Inc. makes every effort to use acid-free ♾, recycled paper ♻.

Book design by Elizabeth Neal

Library of Congress Cataloging-in-Publication Data is on file with the publisher.

ISBN-13: 978-1-60961-488-1   paperback

Distributed to the trade by Macmillan

2   4   6   8   10   9   7   5   3   1   Paperback

RODALE.

We inspire and enable people to improve their lives and the world around them.
rodalebooks.com

For Deborah Atkinson

Always number one in my book,
always there for me, unconditionally,
and for that I am grateful,
and will be, forever.

CONTENTS

CHAPTER 5:

NATURAL SELECTION

It is no coincidence that Ben Hogan won 63 tournaments, including 9 major championships using a custom-fit putter. All things being equal, the golfer who putts with a custom putter tailored to one's comfortably correct setup and natural stroke tendencies will perform best on the greens of any golf course.

CHAPTER 6:

ALL SYSTEMS GO

These tried-and-true principles for setting up and employing all four putting techniques in Ben Hogan's innovative system will help you master the art of hitting short, medium-range, and long on-target putts with maximum distance control.

FOREWORD

John Andrisani and I have been friends for 25 years and, like John, I have a deep passion for golf and an even deeper interest in golf instruction, as a former teaching professional affiliated with the Jim McLean Golf School and a longtime amateur golfer. I now play to a low handicap, having regained my amateur status, yet, just like middle- and high-handicap golfers, I can always use help, especially in the three most important departments of the game: driving, wedge play, and putting. So when John telephoned me to say he was working on a new book on putting, I was intrigued.

But when I learned the book would focus on Ben Hogan, I took particular interest. I was Mr. Hogan's personal assistant in 1981 and 1982. By the time I worked for him, his career as a tour professional was over, yet he still spent a lot of time doing two things, almost daily, that we can all learn from.

Mr. Hogan experimented in practice, typically on the putting green at Shady Oaks Country Club, his favorite Texas spot, doing what he had done his entire career: testing out different putting grips, stances, ball positions, back-and-through paths to swing the putter along—technical nuances of all kinds—looking for something new to add to an already solid system.

Mr. Hogan tweaked his putter in his at-home workshop in Fort Worth, Texas: doing such things as changing the grip to a round grip, paddle grip with flat top and round sides, paddle grip with flat top and flat sides, leather grip, thick chord grip, adding weight to the putter's head, changing the lie and/or loft of the putter, all for the purpose of trying to determine what works best and what can work better than ever.

From observing Mr. Hogan putt, in practice and in play, I would like to add something to John's analysis of the square-to-square stroke, something I know to be Mr. Hogan's mainstay stroke action. Mr. Hogan's secret was making sure that his eyes were over the target line, the same path the club is to travel along. I also learned this from chatting with Mr. Hogan and watching him employ the on-line putting stroke: You do not need to have an upright putter to employ this stroke. Mr. Hogan is using a flat-lie putter, a couple of degrees flatter than standard, on the cover of this book. Just look how square he keeps the putter's face through impact. It just doesn't get any better than that! Another of Mr. Hogan's secrets for employing square and solid contact with the golf ball has to do with a "Double-Overlap" grip he discovered, and which John is going to tell golfers like you about, for the very first time.

Whereas my main interest in any instructional putting book involves discovering new tips that will allow me to employ a more technically correct putting stroke more consistently, *Hogan on the Green* is of special interest to me, owing to my having worked for Mr. Hogan, in what seems a lifetime ago. After reading a late draft of John's book, I felt I had gone back in time, when every day of the week I met Mr. Hogan in his office at 10 o'clock sharp and, whenever possible, I would take a late lunch just so I could watch him practice hitting full shots. If the Texas weather was just a little too hot to hit drives and irons, I'd watch Mr. Hogan practice putting, although a lot of the time he would hit putts when no one was around. And, without giving the book away, let me just tell you why.

As John explains, Mr. Hogan was working on perfecting a revolutionary putting system, and cared so much about getting it right—and "right" meant perfect—even after retiring from competition, that he tweaked it over and over so that golfers could benefit from the secrets he discovered.

Leave it to John Andrisani to reveal the missing link in Ben Hogan's golf game that went unnoticed for decades: a putting system comprised of two main strokes, a square-to-square stroke and an inside-square-down the line stroke, plus an additional hybrid or offshoot stroke for each of these two main strokes.

Ben Hogan was a very talented putter and it is about time someone stepped up to the plate and acknowledged his excellence on the greens. The reason so few ever hear about Mr. Hogan's putting prowess is because it was overshadowed by his sensational swing. For this reason, I'm proud that John is going to take golfers out of the shadows and present them with this new system for putting short, medium-length, and long putts, based on the putting game of Ben Hogan.

Hogan on the Green puts putting instruction on a whole new plane, via an analysis of the techniques of an old master, a genius with an extraordinary skill on the green, a genius that included knowing how to stroke putts in the most efficient and effective manner, even though, admittedly, he sometimes complained about putting or was critical of this department of the game. The truth is, Mr. Hogan did this because he was searching for perfection. And from what the record books show, and from what I learned from reading this book, it seems Mr. Hogan accomplished that goal.

GREG HOOD
January 1, 2013
Carmel, on the Monterey Peninsula, California

INTRODUCTION

William Benjamin Hogan (1912-1997) is recognized, historically, as the most solid ball-striker and on-target tee-to-green player of all time, and I know of no golf fan, swing coach, golf writer, tour golfer, golf historian, country club golf professional, member of a private golf club, public course golfer, caddie, or editor of a leading golf magazine who would argue with such admirable and deserving labels for the late, great golfer. The talented and tenacious silent man from Fort Worth, Texas, chose to let his clubs do the talking— speaking the loudest, if you will, in 1953, when he became the first man ever to win three consecutive major championships in a single year: the Masters at Augusta National Golf Club in Georgia, the United States Open at Oakmont Country Club in Pennsylvania, and The Open Championship (British Open) at the Carnoustie links in Scotland. This would have been an incredible accomplishment for any professional golfer, yet for one who had, 4 years earlier, nearly died in a horrific head-on collision with a Greyhound bus, this phenomenal feat was deemed miraculous, and providing more evidence of the truth behind the words: "God helps those who help themselves."

"I play to win, and I think the Lord has let me win for a purpose," Ben Hogan wrote in an article titled "The Greatest Year of My Life" that appeared in the October 17, 1953 issue of the *Saturday Evening Post*. "I hope that purpose is to give courage to those people who are sick or injured and broken in body."

No pro golfer performed better on the golf course during the 1950s than "The Hawk," a moniker American golf fans affectionately and accurately gave Ben Hogan for his uncanny ability to stare down a target, employ a flawless-looking swing, and fly a golf ball along the precise line visualized originally in his mind's eye.

Ben Hogan thrived on the intensity of championship play. He performed so well under pressure that anyone watching him consistently hit on-target tee-to-green shots and sink putts en route to winning 63 professional tournaments, a record highlighted by 9 major championships, could understand why the Scots nicknamed the diminutive Texan "The Wee Ice Mon."

Frankly, this was a most fitting title, since Ben Hogan possessed something more than cool nerves on the links. He possessed ice in his veins.

Ironically, while the accolades for Ben Hogan kept coming during his heyday (and deservedly so, owing to those unforgettable power-fade drives that split the narrowest of fairways and those approach shots that, on hole after hole, hit the green and sometimes hit the flagstick as many as three times in a round), his prowess with the putter went largely unnoticed by everyone except his inner circle of tour pros and teachers, as well as a few savvy golf aficionados and insiders close to the champion.

Hogan's proficiency with the putter was like no other when it came to sinking different length putts on different putting surfaces, particularly on the tricky and treacherous greens of major championships.

While Hogan's postaccident win in the 1950 U.S. Open at Merion Golf Club was most memorable, his putting skills reached peak levels in that magical year of 1953, when he won all three major championships in which he played. Three years later, Hogan proved that the system of putting he had been developing was working well. It allowed him to sink putts on greens that were giving lots of golfers trouble in the 1956 Canada Cup (now called the World Cup) contested over the very difficult Burma Road course at Wentworth Golf Club in England, owing to greens featuring a mix of subtle and severe breaks, and which rolled at speeds oscillating between fast, slow, and medium-fast. Hogan played his tee-to-green shots to perfection and putted so well at Wentworth that he easily won both the individual title and the team title with his partner, Sam Snead.

All these years later, with the publication of *Hogan on the Green*, the golf world is finally going to learn about this champion's

other skill—putting—a subject Ben Hogan planned to write about in *Five Lessons: The Modern Fundamentals of Putting* as a sequel to his classic instructional text on the swing, *Five Lessons: The Modern Fundamentals of Golf.* Hogan's putting book was never completed, however; in fact, it barely got started. This is a shame, really, considering how members of the press are somewhat to blame for saying that Hogan had contracted a case of "the yips," just because he did what every other great champion has done by missing a couple of makeable putts. Hogan's famed miss in the 1956 U.S. Open, I argue, was due not to any flaw in his mechanics but to his changing to a new putter that was not custom-fit like the trusty brass putter he won with that very same year in the Canada Cup.

"At Oak Hill, trying a new blade putter— Ben had dismissed his old brass model—he missed a number of short ones he would have gobbled up during his peak years," wrote Herbert Warren Wind in *The Story of American Golf,* a book published, ironically, a year prior to *Five Lessons.*

In 1959, at the age of 46, Hogan surprised the sports world by putting his way to a record fifth win at the Colonial in his hometown of Fort Worth. It was after this stunning victory that Hogan made a telephone call to Mr. Wind, his collaborator on *Five Lessons,* to express interest in collaborating on a new book. The subject was not mentioned again until 1960, after Hogan nearly won the U.S. Open at Cherry Hills. He played the last two days of the tournament—ultimately won by Arnold Palmer—with a 21-year-old Jack Nicklaus, who Hogan noticed was putting a lot like he set up and stroked putts himself. Hogan did not share this keen observation with Mr. Wind, yet, once again, the two men talked about collaborating on a new instructional book. Again, there was no follow-up telephone call from Hogan.

In 1967, after Hogan shot a record score of 30 on the back nine at challenging Augusta National at that year's Masters, he placed another telephone call to Mr. Wind. This time it came with a request by Ben for Herb to come down and meet with him in Texas, to discuss a new book.

"I'm also partially to blame [for Hogan's putting book never coming to fruition], having downplayed Ben's putting skills and spectacular performances on the greens, because our book, *Five Lessons: The Modern Fundamentals of Golf,* was coming out . . . never thinking Ben was ever going to write a book on putting . . . a plan I never heard about until 1967," Mr. Wind once confessed to me over dinner.

This new book uncovers for the first time Hogan's lost putting principles, even the first evidence of a new grip Hogan invented, making it an authentic replacement for the book Hogan intended to write about golf's "ground game."

This analysis of Hogan's putting methods, defined most by an innovative four-stroke system, is presented in a simple, easy-to-follow manner and is based on good old-fashioned investigative reporting: casual meetings and formal interviews with true golf insiders—old and new—saw or heard something, directly or indirectly, about Hogan's putting-setup-stroke, strategy, or equipment. Yet they aways lacked the platform to break the story and share the secrets to Hogan's putting success on the greens.

Ben Hogan's scoring records speak volumes about his putting prowess, and all the stories I have pulled into this book—stories culled from my own experiences as well as those of true golf insiders, putting scholars, past and present renowned golf instructors, club and tour professionals, golf magazine editors and publishers, club makers, fans, and friends—make *Hogan on the Green* the definitive word on Hogan's putting system.

While Ben Hogan is considered the best ever model swinger of a golf club and is remembered most for his control of mind, body, drives, and approach shots, he never could have chalked up 63 wins in all, plus won the Vardon Trophy for the lowest stroke average, the Player of the Year award, and finished first on the PGA Tour money list, all multiple times, had it not been for his superb, highly underrated putting game.

Hogan on the Green takes such a detailed look at Ben Hogan's putting game that it can rightfully and justifiably serve as any golfer's guidebook to putting improvement and, possibly, mastery. In this book, golfers will learn how to employ four different putting strokes, composed of two master strokes—a square-to-square action and inside-square-down the line action and two offshoot or hybrid strokes, accented with unique technical nuances related to the elements of grip, stance, club and body alignment, back-stroke and down-stroke, with guidelines for determining which stroke works best in what type of putting situation.

According to surveys I conducted, personal observations, and analysis of data, average public and private club golfers are still doing what they did 25 years ago—putting with fashionable expensive putters, yet ones that, in most cases, are not customized; believing that the same putting stroke will work for all putts; standing at address, ready to trigger the putting stroke and thinking about what can go wrong rather than what to do right; missing a high percentage of short putts and makeable medium-length putts; and three-putting several times per round, especially on putts of over 25 feet.

This book will teach you the ins and outs of working with your local golf pro to customize the putter you now carry in your bag or advise you on what to look for in a new model, while providing you the ultimate reference source: the "specs" of Ben Hogan's favorite putter. In addition, using Hogan as the model prestroke planner, I'll teach you how to read the break, grain, and speed of different greens and how to relax over the ball when setting up to putt, and I'll share the secrets of Ben Hogan's four-stroke putting system. All of this information is based on what Hogan learned from experimental trial-and-error practice and from studying the best putters from past eras, such as Australian amateur Walter Travis, and ace putters of his own time, most notably Bobby Locke, a superb long-range putter and four-time winner of The Open Championship, and Claude Harmon, a deadly short- and medium-range putter and winner of the 1948 Masters. This book also draws insight from conversations and hands-on work with Hogan's club maker, Gene Sheeley, and fundamental putting tips given to Hogan by Dick Grout, the club professional at the Glen Garden Club in Fort Worth, Jack Grout, Dick's brother and assistant pro at "The Garden" (and the man who would go on to teach Jack Nicklaus for most of his career), and, last but not least, Ben Hogan's mentor, tour golfer Henry Picard.

In *Hogan on the Green*, I start where Herbert Warren Wind left off when returning home, a short time after the 1967 Masters Tournament, all excited about the two days of meetings he had with Ben Hogan in Fort Worth and the news he received firsthand about beginning a book on Hogan's proven putting system for handling short, medium-length, and long putts on greens of varying grass textures and speeds.

The focal point of this book, its analysis of Hogan's techniques for putting on fast bent grass greens common in the northeastern United States, slow Bermuda grass putting surfaces prevalent in the southern region of America, and medium-speed poa annua grass greens still quite common on America's West Coast (particularly on oceanside courses such as Pebble Beach, located on the lip of the Pacific Ocean in Monterey, California), is a time-tested, proven system that promotes a solid hit and on-target putts, and, at the same time, prevents putting demons from destroying your golf game.

Hogan on the Green also tells the story of how Ben Hogan worked diligently, before and after 1949—the year of his near-fatal car crash—to crack the code of the putting mystery and discover the secrets to sinking a high percentage of putts per round.

Hogan knew for sure that to develop a consistent putting system was going to be extremely time-consuming and, frankly, a grind mentally, due to the frustration of commonly taught methods failing. All the same,

Hogan faced this challenge head-on, knowing in his heart and head that only by finding a virtually foolproof system—one that would allow him to handle any and all putting green situations and hole putts of varying lengths and varying speeds under pressure—could he shoot more sub-par rounds consistently.

Hogan, who was a graduate with honors from the school of hard knocks, matured early as a player, recognizing the fine line that exists between good putters and great putters. He saw that a player hitting a tee shot can miss the center of the fairway by as much as 50 yards, on a par-four or par-five hole, and still be hitting off the "short grass" with a good angle into the hole for the approach shot. On the green, there is no such luxury. In fact, missing a putt by a mile or by just a fraction of an inch still means a lost stroke. Furthermore, one miss or make per round can represent the difference between losing or winning the Masters, the United States Open, The Open Championship, the PGA Championship, or any regular tour event, for that matter.

Facing up to this reality of golfing life, Ben trimmed down his tournament schedule, sacrificed playing time for practice time, and in his usual methodical manner began to search for not just a better way to putt but the best way to putt. Hogan's search for the truth about what setup and stroke techniques will work best for all golfers led to the discovery of the foolproof four-stroke system at last revealed in this book. His system will help clear golfers' minds of all the smoke-and-mirrors putting instruction proffered by some no-name non-PGA-affiliated golf teachers, as well as the bad advice given to golfers being measured for custom putters by some charlatan "pros" running off-course shops and selling cheaply made knockoffs that fail to measure up to the brand-name models leading PGA Tour and LPGA Tour golfers use to hit and sink the putts their livelihoods depend on.

In *Hogan on the Green*, I share the secrets that brought Ben to the winner's circle time and again, and I map out a clear-cut plan for learning to sink more putts and "going low" on the green.

Over the six main chapters of the book, you'll find instruction on the setup and stroke positions unique to Hogan's putting system, as well as instruction for picking the right putter and what to expect when being fit for a custom putter. I also delve into the mental side of putting—so important to Hogan's success—and go beyond the realm of visualizing the perfect putt. You'll also find helpful anecdotes involving how-to hints Hogan received from the pros at the Glen Garden Club and while playing on tour and working as the tour professional at Hershey Country Club in Pennsylvania. Yet some of the most valuable lessons come in this book's

special insert section, which contains anecdotes ranging from pianist Hoagy Carmichael's unlikely role in helping Ben improve his putting game to the unorthodox practice sessions Hogan partook in, including putting drills done while on the road, in a rented home or hotel room. It also tells of an extraordinary putting tip Hogan once received from Jimmy Demaret, a two-time Masters champion and friend, explains how Jack Burke Jr. helped Ben refine his putting techniques, and explores why Hogan paid so much attention to the putting progress of a young but emerging Jack Nicklaus.

These insights will lead you to spend less time at the driving range and more time on the putting green at your local public course or country club. That's a good thing, since the harder you work at learning and perfecting the four strokes Hogan relied on when winning, the more you will start to see improvement in your putting scores.

As a former PGA affiliated instructor, course record holder, winner of the World Golf Writers' Championship, former longtime senior editor of instruction at *GOLF Magazine,* and author of over 30 golf instruction books, I knew something about putting before beginning my investigation into Ben Hogan's putting methods. And although I expected to learn new things about putting setup and putting stroke positions, I had no idea that Hogan's four putting techniques would be so different and make so much sense, and would allow me to improve my putting skills enough to lead me to make a total switch to this great player's system, which I did after sinking so many more putts and playing consistently on courses featuring bent or Bermuda grass greens.

Now, finally, it's your turn to learn Hogan's incredible four-stroke method. This task will be less daunting if you read this book through once without paying attention to the photographs and artwork, and then read it a second time, just reviewing the photos and art and reading the accompanying captions. Next, I recommend giving the book a day's rest, since it contains such a wealth of new putting information that it is necessary to give your body and mind time to digest everything. Finally, I suggest you read the book all the way through in one long sitting, cross-referencing the text with the pictures and captions.

But before moving on to Chapter 1, you must first choose one of the following three paths to putting improvement:

1. Make the commitment to exchange your existing putting technique for Ben Hogan's various setup and stroke positions, and follow the instructions put forth in *Hogan on the Green* to the letter.

2. Incorporate a few of Ben Hogan's putting actions into your existing stroke so that, ideally, you see improvement—then stop at that point, satisfied with your return on investment.

3. Become so pleased with your progress, according to choice #2 cited above, that instead of stopping you decide to move further along step by step and see where this in-depth analysis of Ben Hogan's innovative and practical system for saving vital strokes on the green takes you.

Please, now go back and read choices 1, 2, and 3 again, more slowly this time and while being more serious about your goals, since I would never want you to neglect your family or your job or business to spend time you cannot afford to spend at the golf course. The good news is that all you need to learn to putt better is a suitable putter, a few golf balls, a place to practice, such as the putting green of a local public course or a living room with a smooth rolling carpet, and some free time.

Whatever choice you make in the end should be based on the present state of your putting game, your realistic goals concerning just how good a putter you want to become, how much leisure time you can devote to practice each week, and how much time you are willing to give yourself before you expect to see noticeable improvements in your putting scores.

Best of luck to you.

—JOHN ANDRISANI

CHAPTER 1
THE PUTTING MYSTIQUE

Ben Hogan once, sarcastically, called putting "another game," but as he matured as a golfer he gained respect for the ground game and the art of rolling the rock with the flat stick.

M y writing career spans 35 years, first as a free-lance writer of golf articles, followed by 5 years working in London as a golf columnist for the *Surrey County Magazine* while working concurrently as an assistant editor of the weekly publication *Golf Illustrated*, the first-ever golf magazine, and last but by no means least, a 15-year stint as senior editor of instruction at *GOLF Magazine*.

During this period of time, I can say, proudly, that I've collaborated with the world's best golf teachers and top tour professionals on instructional articles and how-to books, covering everything from full-swing technique to fairway iron play, from trouble play shots to power-driving methods, from short game to putting tips.

When it comes to putting, I've observed and picked the brains of some the game's most talented and accomplished putters, including Ben Crenshaw, Isao Aoki, Billy Casper, Gary Player, Bob Charles, Jan Stephenson, and Seve Ballesteros, in addition to lesser-known but supremely skilled putters like Morris Hatalsky and John Garner. I have also had the opportunity to work with Dave Pelz, golf's foremost putting guru, and to interview Stan Utley, the famed pro and short game expert, and glean insights from their vast knowledge of the subject.

In wanting to set the record straight as to the truth about Hogan's putting skills, and the historical significance of the innovative four-stroke putting system this talented Texan depended on to hit winning putts and set scoring records in major championships, I did some meditating on the best orthodox and unorthodox methods of the past and present, as Hogan himself had done during the 1930s, 1940s, and 1950s. In the process, I discovered an interesting irony having to do, particularly, with today's popular putting trends.

Once I started seriously looking at all of the present putting styles being pitched as unique, such as the cross-handed technique employed by PGA Tour pro and 2003 United States Open Champion Jim Furyk, and went back in history to examine these methods, I realized that the unorthodox methods being presented as new were, by and large, old hat and merely enjoying a revival. To make my point straightaway, Ben Hogan had even tried the cross-handed putting method, decades before Furyk. What's more, Hogan

Ben Hogan (right) with Byron Nelson (left) and President Dwight D. Eisenhower (center) at Augusta National Golf Club, before the start of the 1953 Masters.

had invented new ways to putt that few golf professionals and golf experts took note of, largely because they lacked the "eye" to spot nuances in Hogan's putting actions and, too, because Hogan's unique, sometimes unorthodox techniques failed to fall in line with the common beliefs and teachings of golf instructors of the day. For these reasons, Hogan's system has never been revealed or written about until now.

After conducting my own focus groups composed of public- and private-course golfers and reviewing data based on surveys conducted by leading golf publications, golf equipment companies, and national golf organizations, I learned that average recreational golfers miss a high number of short putts as well as three-putt from the 25- to 50-feet range a few times per round of 18 holes. Furthermore, except for low handicap players, an infinitesimal number of golfers carry a custom-fit putter in their bag.

At this juncture, I realized it was time to reevaluate putting instruction and revisit an old idea, one that originally popped into my head as far back as 1980, while I was on a business trip to the Isle of Man with a veteran golf writer, Englishman John Stobbs.

While flying over the Irish Sea with John in a prop plane, I brought up the subject of Ben Hogan's incredible power-fade swing, hoping to hear some new insights from a true golf historian and how-to golf expert as well as a single-figure handicap player, but the Englishman surprised me by sweeping right over Hogan's full swing. Instead, Stobbs spoke of the area of the game he believed to be the most important of all shot-making departments—putting—then quickly supported his profound statement with facts, citing Hogan's wins in tournaments and major championships and mentioning specific anecdotes about short, medium-length, and long putts Hogan sank on his way to victory.

While I consider myself well-versed on Hogan's major championship first-place finishes, I admit to being surprised when hearing this longtime die-hard Ben Hogan fan

recount success stories on the greens that, as you'll learn, are high on the list of the most clutch putts holed in the quartet of golf's most prestigious events (commonly referred to as the major championships), all of which the great Ben Hogan has won.

While I knew, for example, that Hogan had won the 1953 Masters, shooting a then-record score of 274, I had no idea he had shattered the old record (set by Ralph

Ben Hogan, winner of The Open Championship (British Open) in 1953, proudly holds the coveted Claret Jug.

Guldahl in 1939 and matched in 1948 by Claude Harmon) by five strokes, owing to sinking putts from everywhere on what many golf aficionados consider, beyond question, the trickiest greens in all of golf. No wonder Hogan said in a posttournament press gathering that it was the best he'd ever played over 72 holes.

What was even more incredible was discovering during my research for *Hogan on the Green* how just 3 months later on the slow greens of Scotland's Carnoustie links, Hogan, in his first appearance at The Open Championship, set a new competitive course record by birdieing the final hole with a solid putt into the center of the cup for a final-round score of 68 and a 4-day total of 282.

Sandwiched between these victories was Hogan's win at the U.S. Open at Pennsylvania's famed Oakmont Country Club, featuring greens so large and lightning-fast that three-putt situations were aplenty among the talented field—except for Hogan, who tamed the beast and beat rival Sam Snead with a five-under-par score of 283 over four rounds.

Because the press and golfing public were mesmerized by Ben Hogan's powerfully accurate driving and fairway play, it came as no surprise that American journalists and British scribes focused on Hogan's flawless swing when writing about these three victories, as well as the six other major championship trophies he took home to Fort Worth. Stobbs,

however, was as fanatical about Hogan's putting feats and ability to adjust to changes in green conditions—namely, speed and slope—as everybody else in golf seemed to be about his full swing. But no matter how well Hogan hit the ball from tee to green, he still had to "finish the hole"—what the great amateur Robert Tyre Jones Jr. deemed the most important aspect of golf—by sinking a putt or putts.

Notably, Stobbs had studied Hogan's career, intending to write a feature story for *ParGolf* magazine dispelling the myth about this great pro golfer Americans named "The Hawk" suffering throughout his entire career from a golf disease known as "the yips," which causes the player to employ a short and quick jab-stroke that sends the ball flying well past the hole, or a tight, restricted stroke that causes the ball to finish well short of the cup.

As I was to learn, Ben Hogan's own sporadic complaints about putts not dropping, even after he shot a low score, and once missing a short putt on the 71st green of the 1956 U.S. Open and then afterward making the mistake of telling the assembled sportswriters that his nerves were shot, triggered a firestorm of bad press.

In fact, Hogan's miss—and I was to find out there was more than one—was due to trying out a new putter with a lie angle that was too flat, even for Hogan, who kept his

Once Ben Hogan achieved his goal of solving the mystery of the golf swing and revealed his secrets first in *LIFE* magazine, with Ben making the perfect swing on its cover, his next major goal was to present a new putting method to America's growing golf audience.

hands quite low and preferred a flat-lie putter. Sadly, not one newspaperman told the truth about Hogan's switch to a new putter that was not custom-fit, like the one he had used for so many years. Thankfully, however, for the record, one distinguished member of the press, Herbert Warren Wind, told the true story and wrote about Hogan's switch to a blade putter in *The Story of American Golf* (1956).

While some less-informed, inexperienced golfers might believe Hogan was afflicted with G.D. (Golfer's Disease), I like to think that golf fans with common sense would back Hogan and dismiss such a false label on the basis of his record of sinking hundreds of critical putts during his illustrious career. Moreover, Hogan was a victim of his own self-inflicted neurosis—perfectionism—that sometimes helped him, by encouraging him to push on at all costs and practice for hours a day, and sometimes hurt him because he was rarely satisfied and believed anything short of perfection wasn't good enough. There's no better example of this characteristic trait, albeit in Freudian and Jungian terms, than the recurring nightmare that caused Hogan to wake up in a cold sweat.

On his way to shooting a perfect score, with 17 straight 1's on the scorecard, and looking to score another hole-in-one while standing on the 18th tee, Ben swings and hits a shot that heads straight for the flag, lands on the green in line with the hole, bounces a couple of times, rolls toward the cup, but then lips out. For Hogan the perfectionist, the results spell disaster.

Surely, this anecdote will allow you to appreciate why Hogan, to some degree, brought on his own bad press concerning his putting, notwithstanding the fact that he could have stopped it had he let the press know he improved his putting skills by inventing a new putting system. He had let the world know he had cured his duck-hook problem by inventing a new swing that he told golfers about in a *LIFE* magazine feature story, then via a *Sports Illustrated* instructional series, and then later in the book *Five Lessons: The Modern Fundamentals of Golf*, published in 1957. But, as you'll learn, there's a legitimate reason Ben didn't make the putting announcement.

So why did Ben Hogan hold back in announcing the new putting system he discovered? I pondered this question more than once during the writing of this book. First and foremost, Ben Hogan wanted to be absolutely certain that his putting system was truly perfected to the maximum and universal in its application. That said, it was not until well after Ben had won a total of 63 golf events that he was absolutely convinced the four-stroke system he invented could work for all golfers and allow the average player, as well as the pro, to become more proficient at hitting different length putts on different types of putting greens. Ironically, the success of Jack Nicklaus, a secret protégé of sorts—a man Ben played quite a lot of golf with—had much to do with Hogan's certainty about his system.

Second, for Hogan's system to help the golfer putt his or her very best, the player's putter must be custom-fit, suited to the player's natural setup and stroke tendencies. The putter's specifications, relating to such vital elements as lie, loft, length, and putter-face angle, must match up with the player's hand position at address (high or low, for example) and with the fit accommodating perfectly the manner in which the player brings the club into the ball (for example, with the hands well ahead of the putter's head).

In consideration of these factors, and knowing that during the 1950s it was unheard of for a major golf manufacturer such as Spalding to offer a made-to-measure club-fitting service to golfers, or even for local club professionals to accommodate more than a few members by customizing a putter as best as possible in the workshop by doing such things as thickening the grip, lengthening the putter, or adjusting the lie and loft in a machine, Hogan believed it best to wait until measuring systems for providing custom putters to the masses were perfected and made more widely available to golfers.

On a related note, Ping was the first company to get a grip on this side of the golf equipment business, starting in the early 1970s. As time went by, more companies jumped on the bandwagon, and more and more custom-club shops started popping up across America. Still, Ping was special because light, balanced, heel-and-toe putters with a bigger sweet spot were the company's original anchor. As the brand grew, more models were added to the line and then, later, unique irons, woods, and wedges.

Today, in the year 2013, golfers are offered various options for being custom-fit for putters, and several companies even specialize in this area. You'll learn a lot more about buying a custom "flat stick" when reading Chapter 5, to the point of even finding out if the putter you are presently using is okay as is, allowing you to move right into learning Ben Hogan's unique four-stroke putting system.

HOGAN WAS so mad at himself for complaining about the greens at various courses he competed on or was about to compete on—as was the case prior to the 1953 British Open at Carnoustie Golf Club in Scotland, when he rudely offered to have lawn mowers shipped over from Texas so that the greens could be cut low and roll at a faster speed, an offer that greatly displeased officials at the Royal and Ancient Golf Club of St. Andrews, the governing body for what golf purists such as myself call The Open Championship—that he practiced hard to adjust, and adjusted so well that he won this premier championship. But what mattered most is that Ben learned the same hard lesson Bob Jones (he hated to be called "Bobby") learned after walking off St. Andrews on his first trip to The Open Championship: Golf is a sport played on an imperfect playing field, and a true golfer must be able to deal with the unexpected and move on, since complaining about golf in Scotland is like chastising the pope in the Vatican, and, furthermore, no one man is bigger than the game.

Hogan, like Jones, apologized, but he was to pay for his sins. Feeling disgraced and disgusted by his comments, Hogan never again played in The Open Championship. And it wasn't until Arnold Palmer became America's ambassador of golf overseas that golf pros from the United States really felt welcomed in the country where golf was first played centuries earlier. Furthermore, even though Ben putted well enough to set a course record at Carnoustie in the final round and to secure victory and win the coveted Claret Jug, his reputation as a damn good putter was thrown out the window, leaving him to be regarded by many proud

Scots as the spoiled and angry American. All the same—and thankfully—to die-hard, veteran Scottish golfers, Hogan would remain the Wee Ice Mon.

Sadly, with Hogan's reputation severely damaged, albeit temporarily, he could not possibly bring the golf world up to speed on his new putting system that, although not yet perfect, was close to perfect. I was reminded of this by my astute traveling companion, Mr. Stobbs, who commented that Ben Hogan's putting skills had to be exceptional to perform so well in The Open Championship, over 72 holes on a course with greens that presented numerous changes in speed, from one putting surface to the next, and the bitter cold affecting the grass.

At this stage of Hogan's life, in the aftermath of being honored with a ticker-tape parade down the streets of New York City (in 1953), Ben pushed forward, remaining positive and thanking the Lord for all the good things in his life. After all, Hogan had proven himself as a professional. He was making good money, spending quality time with his wife, Valerie, enjoying winter golf in Florida at Seminole in Palm Beach, playing with friends such as Claude Harmon, enjoying a couple of martinis after the round while talking oil and stock deals with fellow businessmen, and generally relaxing for a change, after years of chasing a dream and hitting thousands of practice shots—and putts—to have his dream come true and really become a legend in his own time.

As the weather calmed and Mr. Stobbs and I glided through the air, down through the clouds toward land, with Castletown Golf Links in sight, I listened to him recount one more anecdote about Ben Hogan. He cited all the putts Ben and partner Sam Snead sunk to win the Canada Cup in 1956, on the Burma Road course at Wentworth Golf Club in Virginia Water, in the county of Surrey, on some of the fastest and most sloped greens in all of England, especially the third green. Incidentally, Hogan also won the individual title in the 1956 Canada Cup, thanks to accurate play from the tee and from the fairway, and to sinking a bunch of birdie putts en route to an 11-under-par score of 277.

BEN HOGAN'S professional golf career commenced in 1931 yet did not kick into gear until 1940, when he won the Vardon Trophy awarded to the pro with the lowest stroke average. Hogan gained steam in 1941 and 1942, by virtue of twice finishing first on the PGA Tour money list. His career reached new heights after he won his first major championship, the 1946 PGA, rose even higher in 1948 with a first U.S. Open win and a second PGA Championship, then fell into an all-time

low in 1949 following the head-on collision that nearly ended his golf career and his life. Hogan miraculously turned things around in 1950, winning a second U.S. Open and earning Player of the Year honors, got even better in 1951 when he won his first Masters and third U.S. Open, and reached a crescendo in 1953, a year filled with such accomplishment and drama that it brought fans, foes, and fellow professionals to tears after Hogan did what no professional golfer had done before: He won all three major championships he entered—the Masters, U.S. Open, and The Open Championship—and, in the process, proved to golfers that the new swing he had worked so diligently to groove was the most efficient and effective action that produced a super-controlled power-fade shot.

Ben Hogan's performances also proved that a player must putt well to shoot low scores and win a high percentage of tournaments entered. With every win Hogan quietly chalked up another victory for the putting system he continued working on, trying to make it perfect—for himself and all the golfers who would play this great game years and years into the future.

Starting with his first major championship win in 1946 and ending with his final major championship win overseas, in the late summer of 1953, Ben Hogan played in 16 major championships and won 9: 2 Masters, 4 U.S. Opens, 1 British Open, and 2 PGA

Championships. What's even more impressive is this: After recovering from that awful car crash of 1949, Ben won 6 of the first 9 majors he entered.

Still, regardless of Ben Hogan's winning ways, members of the golfing public were so enamored, or rather obsessed, with his ability to set up and swing the same way for an entire round and, along the way, hit tee shot after tee shot and approach shot after approach shot solidly, with a slight degree of left-to-right fade-spin imparted on the ball for maximum control, that Hogan's proficiency with the putter went virtually unnoticed—even during his heyday.

All the golf enthusiasts and golf technique fanatics seemed to talk about was the miracle that allowed Hogan to figure out—while recuperating in the hospital and later at home, waiting for his bruised, battered, and broken body to heal—how to employ a super-controlled power-fade swing, hit a high percentage of drives in the fairway, launch approach shot after approach shot high into the air, the ball spinning with left-to-right cut action, then landing super-softly on the green, shoot low scores consistently, and finish first in golf tournaments, especially major championships.

In 1957, Hogan's collaboration with Wind, *Five Lessons: The Modern Fundamentals of Golf,* was published, featuring lucid, lifelike drawings by renowned illustrator Anthony Ravielli. The book became an instant bestseller and classic that continues to sell well. Furthermore, whereas the timing of Hogan's first instructional book, *Power Golf,* was awful, the timing of *Five Lessons* was right on. Yet, for the record, since Hogan's lessons promised average golfers added distance on drives and iron shots, and on-target accuracy, too, the furthest thing from the golfer's mind was associating Ben Hogan with putting proficiency. This new book was only about the swing, in contrast to *Power Golf,* which included instruction on various aspects of the golf game, even putting.

Power Golf was published first in Great Britain in 1949, the year of Hogan's horrific car crash. Though it was available for the American market by 1951, golfers were uninterested, largely because the golf press corps announced and reannounced that Hogan had already figured out a new and better way to swing and hit a super-controlled power-fade shot, and that he planned on writing about it in a new book. That book, designed to satisfy the recreational golfer's obsession with learning how to hit the ball a long distance off the tee and keep the ball on the short fairway grass, and also destined to fly off bookstore shelves once published, was, of course, the aforementioned classic *Five Lessons: The Modern Fundamentals of Golf.*

Because the swing technique Hogan described in *Power Golf* was outdated by the time the book was published, owing to Hogan's new discovery of the power-fade swing, the majority of golfers did not purchase this instructional text. Those that did likely tossed it in the garbage before even finding out that although the swing information in *Power Golf* was anachronistic, the book included some putting tips that all golfers would find helpful. Nevertheless, since Hogan was just starting to unravel the mystery of golf's ground game when he wrote *Power Golf*, much of the instruction was thin and not thought through.

Whereas *Power Golf* was poorly thought out editorially, with pitching, chipping, bunker play, and putting having nothing at all to do with power, *Five Lessons* was on point, concentrating only on the technical elements of Hogan's power-fade money shot, published when Ben was fresh off a darn good long run of playing winning golf. Moreover, *Five Lessons* was met with a warm welcome by low-handicap players plagued by the sharp-turning right-to-left duck-hook shot and high-handicap players who tend to hit a push-slice shot off the tee, a shot that starts flying to the right of target then turns farther right toward the end of its flight. To both categories of player, hitting a

> After recovering from that awful car crash of 1949, Hogan won 6 of the first 9 majors he entered.

controlled power-fade, at will, would be a welcome change.

Five Lessons is divided into just five clearly defined chapters—"The Grip", "Stance and Posture", "The First Part of the Swing", "The Second Part of the Swing", "Summary and Review"—and contains simple, easy-to-follow swing tips. Thus, even today, with the book in its umpteenth printing, players who read it and follow Hogan's advice improve their power driving and driving accuracy skills rapidly. This, from day one, has always been the case, which is one reason *Five Lessons* created such a buzz and a sizzling-hot run on books when first published.

The more golfers that purchased the book, the bigger the buzz among sportswriters, editors of popular golf magazines, golf teachers at private country clubs and public courses across America, novices learning the game at driving ranges, low-handicap golfers looking to get down to scratch, middle-handicap players searching for ways to shoot a score under 80 for the first time, and high-handicap players looking to break 100 or perhaps 90.

Hogan won more major championships between the years 1950 and 1957 than any other pro golfer. With television entering more and more homes across the country by that time, the public sometimes got to see Hogan consistently land his drives in the center of the fairway, hit approach shots onto the greens, and during the four rounds of a tournament sink a high percentage of putts. After the publication of *Five Lessons*, Hogan continued to swing the club beautifully, and although he limited his schedule, he still could do more than hold his own among the younger golfers on tour, winning the 1959 Colonial National Invitational Tournament for a record fifth time and coming close to winning three more major championships. Consequently, *Five Lessons* continued to sell, eventually reaching the number one spot in all-time sales for a golf book.

The credit for communicating the instructional messages in *Five Lessons* goes to Hogan's collaborator, Herbert Warren Wind. The voice is captured brilliantly, plus delivered so honestly, authentically, and intimately by Mr. Wind that for over 50 years readers of the book have commented that they actually felt like Ben Hogan was standing on the driving range or on the tee giving them personal lessons on how to hit a highly desirable power-fade. Notably, it was Mr. Wind whose praise of my own collaboration with Seve Ballesteros, 1988's *Natural Golf*, contributed to the eventual creation of this book.

While talking at length about Ballesteros the man and Ballesteros the master shotmaker over a fine steak dinner with Wind, I first brought up the subject of golf's mental side, stating that, like Hogan, Seve put himself into a trance during the most prestigious tournaments, featuring the most competitive fields, namely, the majors. Seve had confessed to me that about a month prior to the start of each year's Masters, U.S. Open, Open Championship, and PGA Championship, he entered a bubble of concentration—a sacred place the Spanish superstar could be at peace, play with no distractions, and, once reaching a green, visualize certain paths to the hole, depending on the tempo of the stroke and how hard he intended to hit the ball. He visualized all of this in his mind's eye before he actually triggered any stroke, so he could work out within his bubble which stroke was the easiest to repeat under pressure, which stroke was the least bit risky according to the type of grass on the green and the green's condition, and which stroke would work best according to the state of a match with an opponent or what position Seve was in at any particular moment in a standard 72-hole stroke-play championship.

I had mentioned the bubble in *Natural Golf*, but because I had written about it in more general terms, I could tell that Mr.

Wind wanted to learn more. However, he first was just as eager, I could tell, to tell me that Ben Hogan admitted to rehearsing the correct putting action in his head before starting the actual stroke.

The two of us exchanged stories throughout dinner, going back and forth, with me telling Seve stories and Wind sharing Hogan anecdotes. Since Seve's imagination seemed to intrigue the famous writer, I shared the following anecdote with him:

During the writing of *Natural Golf*, I asked Seve to give the reader a detailed, rather than general, sense of what he meant when he talked of seeing several shots play out in his mind, such that he could determine which one would work best, and then go ahead and play it so well.

"Seve," I asked, "what's it like imagining a shot? Do you actually see yourself hitting the ball and watching how it behaves in the air and on the ground?"

"It's like looking at a beautiful, well-dressed woman and knowing exactly what she looks like naked, without her taking off a single piece of clothing," Seve responded.

Wind was amused by the story, although I knew he would certainly not be using it in the column he wrote in *The New Yorker*. I didn't use it in the book either, feeling it was just a little too chauvinistic and too much for the conservative golfers in the United States. Besides, even if I wanted to, Seve's agents,

Jorge de Ceballos and Joseph Collett, would not have permitted it, for fear of losing a multi-million-dollar client.

Returning to the subject of putting, I explained to Wind that although Seve putted with the toe end of the putter off the ground and angled upward, into the air—since that gave him a sense of security that the sweet spot of the putter's face, located nearer its neck and not in its center, would contact the back center portion of the ball (or upper-left quadrant if applying left-to-right cut-spin to the ball)—Seve's more natural method of controlling the back and through strokes with the right hand was also similar to Hogan's putting action.

Before going on, I should mention something Gene Sarazen, the inventor of the sand wedge and multiple major championship winner, wrote in his book *Thirty Years of Championship Golf* (1950), because it gives us our first hint that Ben Hogan had discovered some secrets to good putting. "Anybody can hit the ball," Sarazen wrote. "It takes a golfer to put his shots together, and a three-foot putt is every bit as much of a golf shot as a 250-yard drive. The putter is the big dipper. It separates the cream from the milk. The great champions have all been beautiful putters—Walter Travis, Jerry Travers, Hagen, Jones, Nelson, and Hogan. A champion cannot remain a champion if his putting falls off."

I EXPLAINED to Wind that I was interested in examining Ben Hogan's putting stroke further because it was the most natural, even more so than Seve's, and totally tension-free because Hogan got his arms to bend and relax more by letting his elbows hug his hip bones, depending more on free wrist action.

But as natural as Hogan's putting stroke was during his heyday of the late 1940s and early 1950s, and to a lesser degree stretching all the way to 1967, it differed greatly from the putting stroke taught by 95% of golf instructors I'd interviewed and collaborated with on instruction articles. This puzzled me, because, as I explained further to Wind so many golf instructors teach golfers the swing Hogan proved worked so well and popularized that you would think they'd all be teaching their students how to putt like Hogan, too.

"The reason they don't do that," Wind said, "is simply because the majority don't understand Ben's putting technique. I can tell, already, that you do, just by you picking up on the fact that Hogan was, and still is, a right-sided putter, even though he doesn't play competitively any longer."

I thanked Mr. Wind for his gracious comment and let him know that what he said about teachers certainly applied to those who lacked the years of experience necessary to develop an eye for deconstructing a putting stroke and isolating all of its critical components.

I believed veteran teachers had decided that it was of little use to study Hogan's putting methods when the golfing public had been misled into believing Hogan was just an average-to-good putter who sometimes got really hot on the greens or, conversely, fell into a slump period, only reemerging into the winner's circle after being cured, albeit temporarily, by one of his mentors, most likely Henry Picard or Jack Burke Jr. I added, in conclusion, that it was such a shame teachers felt this way because Ben Hogan's right-sided putting actions were so natural-feeling that they could be repeated easily by feel with just a little bit of steady practice.

AUSTRALIAN-BORN golf instructor Peter Croker is, like Hogan, a right-side advocate and believes in a pushing action to control the putting stroke and the swing because it's more natural. He goes so far as to start a new student off by teaching putting first.

"Putting teaches you how to develop essentially the very same hand and arm action you will use in the full swing," Croker wrote in his book *Peter Croker's Path to Better Golf.* "Just as in the swing, when you allow a pushing action to control the down-stroke in putting, with the goal of both wrists fully unhinging through impact, it is easier to deliver the putter squarely into the ball—consistently."

I found this fascinating, considering how when Hogan was recovering at home from his car crash of 1949, he was anxious to begin solving the mysteries of the golf swing and developing a new action that would eliminate the duck-hook problem he experienced from time to time. There was one problem: Because early on Hogan was still too weak and sore to swing, he switched to testing out some new things he figured out about putting while in the hospital; this, ultimately, became the four-stroke system I write about in this book. So in sorting out his putting game, it is easy to make a logical jump here and conclude that this order of learning, à la the Peter Croker way, likely helped Hogan develop his consistent, super-controlled swing. By accident or because of exceptional instincts, Ben Hogan was once again ahead of his time.

Wind agreed that one chief reason Ben Hogan's basic putting technique is ideal for the average golfer looking to improve his or her skills on the green is because Ben demanded that the right wrist hinge back freely on the back-stroke. Wind agreed that this, too, would be a welcome change for Mr. and Mrs. Average, since in observing hundreds of private- and public-course golfers,

he saw that the majority had great difficulty doing what almost all instructors recommend, which is "keep the wrists locked throughout the putting stroke and control the back-and-through movements of the stroke with the big muscles of the arms and shoulders."

Ben Hogan obviously realized early on that this advice sounds great in theory but in practice is difficult to employ. Moreover, just in case you have yet to try this popularly taught method, it feels unnatural, creates tension in the arms and shoulders, and requires weeks to learn and train your body to execute. However, because the all-arms putting method calls for the wrists to be locked, the golfer tends to hold the putter with what veteran golf instructor Jim McLean calls a "death grip." Consequently, with the pressure in the fingers and palm at 10 on a scale of 1 to 10 that goes from light to firm, one's feel for the swinging club is lost, and the tempo of the stroke is thrown off; such faults prevent the player from being able to sense the distance of the putt through his or her hands and hit the ball the proper distance.

You can now see why Ben Hogan wrote in *Power Golf* that he putts "with my arms, hands, and wrists"—and why, once he had perfected his system, he had such a great feel for judging distance and pacing the ball to the hole, even when hitting long-range putts on super-fast greens.

Hogan's way of controlling the stroke with his right arm, right hand, and right wrist made perfect sense to top-notch golf professionals and real students of the game like Henry Picard, Jack Burke Jr., and Claude Harmon. Although not purely as right-sided as Ben when employing the putting stroke, they had all learned through trial and error that the popular adage spouted by so many golf instructors—"Golf is a game of opposites, so natural right-handers will do better in all departments of shot-making by letting the left side control the motion of the swing and putting stroke"—does golfers more harm than good.

In the hickory shaft days of the early 1900s, greats like Harry Vardon, Edward (Ted) Ray, and John H. Taylor were forced to control their putting strokes with the less dominant left hand. If they didn't, they would tend to release the right wrist early in the down-stroke, such that the hickory shaft—which flexed on the back-stroke—would spring forward in the hitting area and, in a split second, propel the putter face hard into the golf ball at high speed, relatively speaking. As a result, all distance control was lost and the ball would be sent flying well past the cup—or off the green!

Since Ben Hogan was fortunate to play in the era of steel shafts, and wanted the putter to do a lot of the work, he advocated moving the fewest number of body parts in a putting stroke as possible, and putting with an extra-stiff shaft, albeit one tapered down dramatically toward the end nearest the putter's neck, so he'd feel some flex on long putts over short putts. That's what you want to strive for when putting, simply because feel or touch transmitted through the putter's shaft is more essential for judging distance on long-range putts than on short-range putts.

On short putts, Hogan discovered, both in practice and during play, that direction and not distance control is the priority. Therefore, feeling distance through the hands is less of a factor than feeling the "oneness" between your right arm, wrist, and hand, as well as the putter. Consequently, a firm shaft will work best.

Since steel shafts became legal in 1930, according to the rules of golf established and enforced by the United States Golf Association and The Royal and Ancient Golf Club of St. Andrews, there have been some

> On short putts, Hogan discovered, both in practice and during play, that direction and not distance control is the priority.

darn good left-sided putters. But, frankly, the best putters have been those who relied as much on the left hand as the right hand. The simplest explanation for this is that, for right-handed golfers, the left hand controls the direction of the ball and the right hand controls the distance the ball travels across the green. So you can understand why a 100% pure right-sided putter like Ben Hogan was considered a rebel in his day, by all but savvy golfers, most notably a young Jack Nicklaus, who obviously realized, early on, the benefits of a more natural right-sided putting stroke for controlling distance and direction.

It was part of my job as senior instruction editor at *GOLF Magazine* to study new trends and new teaching methods relative to any aspect of the game, including putting, since this area of golf, according to putting expert Dave Pelz, makes up 43% of the shots hit during a round of 18 holes. You can imagine, then, that a large part of my job was spent on the telephone or traveling to golfing destinations, talking to golf teachers and tour professionals about what was new in the world of instruction, in the hope that I would be introduced to a new tip or theory that could be turned into a blockbuster cover story or an instructional article and, in the process, help our readers play a better game and, in turn, lower their handicap.

In fact, it was during one of my earliest

trips to Orlando, to cover Arnold Palmer's Bay Hill Classic, that I noticed something strange. With the exception of Ben Crenshaw and a few other superb putters on the PGA Tour, the majority of the pros were not allowing their right wrists to hinge slightly on the back-stroke and unhinge on the down-stroke. Moreover, not one pro golfer was doing all of the things Ben Hogan did when setting up to putt and stroking (and holing) putts.

In addition to an unnatural left-sided putting action that triggered serious putting flaws and, in turn, caused tour pros to miss putts, shoot higher scores, and lose money and status, many less-informed golf teachers in America were also unknowingly feeding amateur golfers misinformation on what was required to become a good putter. More important, as I explained to Wind, an entire set of new fundamentals, based on Ben Hogan's model putting techniques, needed to be stated and explained, because many of the young tour pros hadn't figured out what Hogan found to be true: that feel is enhanced by employing a right-sided putting stroke, and this directly translates to more putts holed.

BUTCH HARMON, one of the game's foremost instructors, also shared some of his

Hogan secrets in *The Four Cornerstones of Winning Golf*, a part biographical, part instructional book I collaborated on with him. Here—from an interview I conducted with him at the Bay Hill Club in Orlando, Florida—Harmon recalls his observations from an afternoon on the course with Hogan and Hogan's close friend, Butch's dad, Claude Harmon, which he referred to as "the round of a lifetime":

> "One of the most impressive features of Ben Hogan's putting game was the amount of time Ben spent figuring out the breaks in the greens and how his concentrative mind-set intensified once over the ball, as he settled into the address—weight left, elbows tied to the body, eyes glaring, looking at the hole then back down at the ball—and readied himself to start the putting stroke. I could see, even in this friendly game, by the way Mr. Hogan stared at the line to the hole, the wheels in his head turning slowly, steadily, and seriously, how he earned the nickname The Hawk."

What I found so fascinating about conducting research for this book is how many "guest" golf insiders partook in setting the record straight about Ben Hogan's putting game and offered valuable insights.

Take the subject of equipment. While expecting to learn everything about Hogan's putting equipment from Hogan's personal and company clubmaker, Gene Sheeley, that was not the case.

In speaking with Hogan's personal assistant, Greg Hood, who worked for the Ben Hogan Golf Company and Slazenger, I learned some interesting things about the specifications of Hogan's favorite putter, a center-shafted model featuring a head made from a brass doorknob. For example, Hogan alternated between a leather grip with a "paddle" feature that allowed both of his thumbs to lay perfectly flat atop the handle and, in turn, helped keep the club on-line during the stroke, and a coarse-textured chord-line grip, normally used by players on their woods and irons. Hogan had made this grip really fat by having layers of tape added underneath it, in order to eliminate any gap between the fingers and the handle that could cause slippage and move the club off-line during the stroke. At one point, Hogan took it upon himself, doing some club making at home, to lengthen the shaft of his old faithful putter by adding a wooden dowel at the end farthest from the putter head, then regripped the club. This change encouraged Hogan to set up with better posture and, in turn, release any body tension that creeped in during the pressure of playing in a major championship.

The great Sam Snead, winner of a record 81 PGA Tour events, a total of 7 major championships, and over 100 tournaments worldwide, also provided me with a wealth of insightful information on Ben Hogan's putting, and was one of the few persons I interviewed who noticed how Hogan scrutinized other players on tour who were good putters. This bothered Snead and he let Hogan know it, although from time to time they would talk about and help each other with putting—that is, when one wasn't ribbing the other.

"Ben always was looking for an edge, because he was extremely competitive and hated to lose," Snead said. Snead also made the point of telling me that Ben was such a perfectionist, he got so tied up with the early planning and filming stages of the movie about his life, *Follow the Sun*—even the screenplay and casting—that his plans to write a comprehensive putting book instead turned into a short chapter on putting in *Power Golf*, which is the last place one would expect to find such instruction. According to Snead, plans for the putting book were put on hold, and instead Hogan put together all of his notes on putting—keys he kept in a memo pad and sometimes referred to before the round or in between nines—and more or less listed them, albeit with some elaboration, in *Power Golf*.

"Ben, who used to pick my brain because I'd already written books, was such a control man about his shot techniques being portrayed accurately in the movie, with Glenn Ford playing his part, that he insisted on

standing in and hitting some shots in the movie, owing to Ford's techniques not being all that great," Snead said. "But boy, oh boy, did Ben hate the fact that each movie take took so long to set up."

AFTER WRITING *Power Golf* (1949) and *Five Lessons* (1957), Hogan swore he would never get involved with another time-consuming book project, but he was so happy about his win at Colonial in 1959 that he let Wind know of his strong interest to work on another instructional project. He asked Wind if he'd like to sit down and discuss it in private, yet at that stage Hogan said nothing of the subject matter, made no reference to the putting chapter in *Power Golf*, and "provided me no date to meet," Wind recalled. As far as Wind could gather, this creative idea was still in its incubation stage. When Hogan was serious enough to talk about the nature of the book and, more important, begin the project, his collaborator would be ready and willing to do his part.

The next time Hogan called Wind was in the summer of 1960, at which time he kind of said the same thing about wanting to write another book but, again, there was no mention of the subject.

This time, all Hogan wanted to talk about

was the thrill of playing with Jack Nicklaus, a young man he predicted would be the next great golfer. The 20-year-old Nicklaus and the 48-year-old Hogan played together in that year's U.S. Open at Cherry Hills Country Club in Denver, and, as if the script were written by a Hollywood screenwriter, both were in contention to win the championship, what would have been Jack's first major and Hogan's record fifth U.S. Open title. At the end of the second round, they were tied at 142, two under par, and after three rounds the old master and the young gun remained tied, both having shot 69.

On the 71st hole, with a chance to win, Hogan violated his own strategic rule by gambling with a wedge shot over water rather than playing the percentages. Instead of landing the ball well beyond the pin and spinning it back toward the hole, Hogan attempted to land the ball between the water hazard and the pin—located very near the edge of the hazard—and roll the ball to the hole. His shot finished short of the green, and although he was able to salvage bogey, he finished out of first place, as did Nicklaus. Arnold Palmer, spurred on by his "army," drove the first green and scored birdie, then went on to fire his most famous last round score of 65, erasing a 7-stroke deficit to steal the championship.

Nicklaus did set a record for low amateur score, but more than that he learned that when in contention to win, you should respect the difficulty of the course and the challenges it presents, play the course as you normally would, remain patient and confident in your game, and let the birdies come as a result of your fine play. Hogan tried to force a birdie, a mistake akin to the ones young and over-the-hill boxers make. Instead of bobbing, weaving, jabbing, punching the opponent's body over and over to wear that fighter down, the boxer goes for an early knockout and gets caught with an uppercut.

Ben Hogan's jaw was intact, but his spirit was weakened. Jack Nicklaus congratulated him anyway for his fine play and good sportsmanship, and when the two men walked off the last green, the scene was right out of *Casablanca*, for it was, indeed, the start of a beautiful friendship. Hogan would never win another golf tournament, but that did not stop Nicklaus from realizing Hogan was still a model player with a firm grasp of the total game. Nicklaus was savvy enough to play as much golf as possible with Hogan, all the time visually eavesdropping. And after taking a lesson from fellow tour pro Jack Burke Jr., in 1962, on the grip and push-action down-stroke trigger—elements of the putting setup and stroke that Nicklaus found out Hogan had Burke help him refine at Augusta in 1960, and that he learned years earlier when studying amateur golfer Walter Travis—Nicklaus really paid attention.

"I've had the pleasure of playing quite a number of rounds with Ben Hogan since that day in Denver (at the 1960 U.S. Open at Cherry Hills, when the two of us played the final two rounds together)," Nicklaus wrote in his autobiography, *The Greatest Game of All: My Life in Golf.* "At the Masters, for example, we always play at least one practice round together. He names a day and we go out and play. I always learn something from watching Hogan."

The similarities in Hogan's and Nicklaus's putting techniques are striking, with both players holding the handle of the putter with a weak left-hand grip and strong right-hand grip; both setting their eyes over the target line behind the ball on short putts; the same crouched address position, open stance, and bent arms at address with the elbows pointing outward; and the same push-action with the right palm and forearm employed to propel the ball along a designated line. Again, Hogan first learned this push-action from viewing old photographs of Walter Travis and later refined it, in 1960, during Masters week, with the help of Jack Burke Jr. Nicklaus, according to what he wrote in his book *Golf My Way* (1974), was taught this same right-sided push-action by Burke, but 2 years after Hogan. Burke also convinced Nicklaus to try a new weaker left-hand grip position, with the thumb pointing straight down the putter's handle, and a strong right-hand grip,

with the hand turned more under the shaft. This hold, which Nicklaus used from that point on during his illustrious career, was a clone of Ben Hogan's.

Burke and Hogan exchanged ideas frequently on putting technique and spent quite a bit of time together on the putting green, during Masters week particularly, but also when playing together or meeting for lunch at either Champions, the club Burke built with Jimmy Demaret in Houston, or Shady Oaks Country Club, Hogan's home base in Fort Worth.

While Hogan's basic setup and stroke were similar to the address position and putting action employed by Nicklaus, Jack, for whatever reason, did not completely clone Hogan's hinge and rehinge action of the wrists, and Hogan told the late, great golf writer Charles Price that if Jack had copied him, he would have been an even better putter, as the club face-to-ball contact would have been more solid. This theory proved true because although Nicklaus is generally believed to be the greatest putter of all time from 5 feet and in on the fastest and most sloping greens, he often missed short from 10 feet and out. Now, some of you will say that I'm criticizing the great Nicklaus unfairly because during his career he was a die putter. That's true. He did, like Bob Jones, prefer to let the ball slow down by the hole so that it had a chance of falling into the front door, back door, or either of the side doors. Hogan was a die putter, too, but he never played lottery games like that when hitting putts measuring around 10 feet in length. Rather, he stepped up and hit the ball solidly into the cup. By that, I do not mean Hogan banged the ball into the cup, which is almost as bad as hitting it too softly; I mean that Hogan stroked the putt authoritatively, at a slightly faster speed, by releasing and straightening the right wrist a little faster than normal.

I believe Hogan was able to sink these putts a high percentage of the time because of what he did that Jack Nicklaus did not do—and I'm not talking about Jack's failing to use his wrists properly. That's a result, not a cause. What caused Jack to not be able to acquire some added feel through the wrist hinge, even a slight cocking of the right wrist (which, by the way, he did do on long putts), was that his arms and shoulders were tense. This body freeze was what caused his wrists to lock up and, in turn, the club to be swung at a slower speed and, as a result, the ball to come up short of the hole.

Ben Hogan's hinging and straightening actions of the wrists are unique and will certainly help those whose medium-range putts tend to fall short of the hole, provided the player grips the club lightly enough to have good feel for the putter, yet firmly enough for a secure grip that allows the putter to swing straight back and straight

through along the target line, in one smooth, uninterrupted motion, with no fear of it moving off the correct path. Furthermore, when the grip is good and the timing of the wrist action is in sync with the movement of the putter, the ball will be struck solidly and hold its line all the way to the hole.

When working on *Natural Golf* with Seve Ballesteros, and spending many hours interviewing and playing golf with this great player, I asked him one day, during a discussion of his setup, about holding the club slightly above the grass rather than soling the bottom of the club head, its "sole," on the ground, as Jack Nicklaus does when addressing the ball with every club in his bag, including his putter. Seve said that he was against this because he believed it adds tension to the arms and thus has the potential to play havoc with the swing and putting stroke. He shared that insight with Nicklaus, and Jack responded by telling Seve, albeit diplomatically, that others had told him the same thing previously. Soling the club worked well for Nicklaus, and that is all that mattered to him.

Jack is right, and Ben Hogan would never argue with what works. The fact is, however, if you are going to go all out and copy Hogan's putting techniques, then, based on my years of expertise in golf instruction, you cannot mix apples and oranges. Ken Venturi, the 1964 U.S. Open champion and close friend of Hogan's, told me that Hogan was dead against holding the club head above the grass, on putts especially, because this unorthodox setup position leads to an exaggerated arms-controlled stroke and an overly slow tempo, and results in putts coming up short of the hole. Venturi added that the same result comes from gripping the putter too tightly. Hearing these comments, I bet that one of the pros that criticized this aspect of the Nicklaus setup was Ben Hogan himself, likely during a practice round with Jack, or afterward while relaxing over a drink at the 19th hole.

Ben Hogan's hinging and straightening actions of the wrists are unique and will certainly help those whose medium-range putts tend to fall short of the hole.

Throwing my own analytical two cents in, I'm definitely not in favor of Jack's way of setting up with his head behind the ball and eyes over the target line on all putts. This position was something Hogan experimented with himself and found it worked well on short putts, since it actually encourages an on-line stroke. Yet it's an address position Hogan would never recommend for long putts. The reason is that this setup promotes too straight a stroke path for putts over 25 feet, whereas standing back with one's head over a spot between the target line and the body promotes the proper inside action and a purely paced putt. All the same, you must guard against setting the eyes over a spot too far inside the target line or else the putting stroke will become too flat, and thus the putter's face cannot be returned to a square impact position without some degree of manipulation with the hands and wrists. The more I think about this feature of Jack Nicklaus's address position, the more I'm convinced that this is the reason Jack was always an excellent short-distance putter and a less-than-excellent long-range putter, in comparison to the greats, whereas in his day Tom Watson, Jack's chief rival, was someone Ben considered among the very best from long range, as every fan of what Americans call the British Open will attest. En route to winning five British titles (and very nearly a sixth at age 59), Tom sunk a heck of a lot of long putts, although the one Nicklaus holed on the 18th in their 1977 battle royale at Turnberry, in Scotland, was something else.

As a matter of further interest, I'm sure it's no coincidence that Ben Hogan's top-ranked long putter was Bobby Locke, winner of four

British Open championships, who, like Watson, imparted sidespin on the ball when putting on greens slower than those on American courses. Locke, however, went so far as to impart a touch of hook-spin on putts when the greens were really slow. In fact, it was a form of this same countermeasure technique that helped Hogan sink putts on the slow greens at Carnoustie en route to setting a course record and winning the 1953 British Open.

BETWEEN 1963, when he won his first major, and 1967, the year he was named the PGA Player of the Year, Jack Nicklaus won seven major championships. But 1967 was also a big year for Hogan, as "The Hawk" did something really big that year, especially for a 55-year-old golfer. He shot a 30 on the back nine at Augusta National, setting a new Masters record, thanks to accurate tee shots, on-target iron shots, but most of all, putts holed on the truest yet fastest greens in the world. Most impressive about Hogan's performance at the 1967 Masters was the four consecutive birdie putts he sank on holes 10 through 13, four extremely challenging holes known to golf aficionados as Amen Corner (as so dubbed by Herbert Warren Wind). Those who try to convince them-

selves, as so many brash young PGA Tour players have to their great detriment, that this quartet of holes is like any other, find themselves living a moment right out of Dante's *Inferno.*

Take hole number 12, called "Golden Bell," a par-three requiring only some species of short iron to hit the green and two putts for par. Year after year, without fail, this hole causes players to miss the cut and on Sunday, when the final round is played to decide the winner, it kills off more. The reason is that, having committed the mortal sin of not allowing for a headwind that's hard to detect from the tee (since the tall loblolly pines behind the green often stop the flag from moving), players often hit balls that fly high yet fall short of the green, splashing into Rae's Creek or landing on the shaved bank of grass and then rolling back down into the same body of water fronting the green. Sometimes, too, a player—usually one making his first trip to Augusta—will select too strong a club, figuring the wind is up, swing a little hard, and send the ball flying over the green, over the back bunker, into bushes and sandy terrain.

Once on this green or any of the others around Amen Corner, I'm sure at least one golfer playing this course as a guest felt compelled, after the round, to scan the Internet or to telephone the Royal Geographical Society in London or to call *National*

Geographic to check and see if this beautiful course, which we know was originally a nursery, has roots that go farther back and perhaps was, thousands of years ago, part of the Himalayas.

I say this in jest of course, because Augusta is truly a heavenly place with beautifully manicured greens. Yet these greens are severely sloped, and so slick that four-putts are not unusual, even during the Masters when the game's best are competing, simply because if you hit a putt a little too easy or a little too hard, you'll find yourself in a lot of trouble. I bring this up because so many who watch the Masters each year on television cannot appreciate how sloped the greens of Augusta National are, and to prove a point about Hogan's accomplishment at Augusta that, once and for all, quieted all the fools who started and ran with the rumor about him suffering from a serious case of "the yips." Fortunately, anyone who really knows golf knows that "the yips," as top teacher David Lee wrote in his book *Gravity Golf,* "are not caused by bad nerves, but improper mechanics."

Ben Hogan, the ultimate technician, positioned his eyes directly over the target line, behind the ball, when hitting short and medium-range putts, as this position helped him keep the putter's face square to the hole as it moved back and forth along the target line, from start to finish. More important,

Dave Pelz believes this straight-back straight-through putting stroke is best. The bottom line is that Hogan depended on pure and proper mechanics for this type of stroke and for all the techniques in the four-stroke putting system he invented and really never stopped perfecting.

In the 1967 Masters, following his four straight birdies stretch, Hogan finished the job by scoring par on hole 14, birdieing 15, sinking par-saving putts on 16 and 17, and scoring a birdie three on 18 with another solid putt, to arrive at that record back nine score of 30. Hogan, so pleased with his play under pressure—especially his birdie barrage on the back nine, when his mind, body, and putter all blended together harmoniously thanks to a tip he received a year earlier when playing with Jack Nicklaus—decided to permanently incorporate the tip into his putting system.

Observing Nicklaus putting during a practice round together in 1966, Hogan noticed Nicklaus employed a "forward press" action of the hands, moving them a tad toward the hole, with the shaft following. A split second later, albeit via a smooth transition, Jack started the putter back, rhythmically, at an even, controlled pace. As he proved then and during 18 major championships, when you start that way, you greatly increase your chances of returning the putter's face squarely into the ball, rolling the ball smoothly along the correct line toward the hole, and sinking the putt.

Ben believed Jack's forward press move could help a golfer make a smoother start to the stroke and, in turn, promote an overall fluid and rhythmic action—that is, with the caveat that the "forward press" be deliberate, never rushed.

Regardless of his advancing age and his lack of touch relative to his younger days on tour, I was certain that Hogan's accomplishment at the 1967 Masters had signaled to him, at last, that his unique putting system worked. I also felt confident that Hogan must have realized at the time that this performance proved that the putting strokes in his system—all four of them—operated essentially on automatic pilot. He had discovered the secret to letting the club do the work, the dream of every golfer, pro or amateur, low-, high-, or middle-handicapper. But was Hogan convinced he had discovered the Holy Grail of putting instruction?

According to Herbert Warren Wind, the answer is no. "Ben was still not convinced," Wind told me. "I thought he was after I returned from spending two days with him in Texas, at his home, after he had summoned me down in 1967, around a fortnight or so after he shot that incredible record inward nine score at Augusta, to talk about a new book on putting that he wanted me to collaborate on, and that he

wanted me to speak to Jack Nicklaus about writing an introduction for, because of the similarities between his putting setup and stroke and Jack's, the fact that both had taken lessons from Jack Burke, and [he felt] Jack's endorsement would add credibility to the book. Ben was gung-ho because I had worked with him on *Five Lessons* but also because he knew I kept close tabs on the career and techniques of Jack Nicklaus, whose biography, *The Greatest Game of All*, included instruction on putting I believe I'd already started researching."

Mr. Wind was alerted to hold back, however, about 2 weeks after his Texas meeting, when Ben said he wanted to meet again, this time with artist Anthony Ravielli present, since he wanted to make sure Tony had the time and the inclination to do illustrations on putting, in the same style he employed when illustrating *Five Lessons*. Ben was also relieved to learn that Wind had not yet called Nicklaus. The telephone call ended with Hogan telling Wind he would be in touch to propose a meeting date.

After about a month, having heard nothing more about any meeting to discuss the new book on putting, Wind contacted Ravielli. Wind had already seen two of the drawings Ravielli intended to bring to the meeting, and he worried about how many more he might have done. Fortunately, Ravielli had put the project on hold, too, having not heard from Wind.

Eventually, Hogan did call, confirming that he wanted to wait, since he still was not convinced that his system was ready for publication. At that point Wind stopped conducting research, which he said was a shame, because he was surprised when going back in time, even going back and looking at his own books, how many clutch putts Hogan had sunk to set records and win major championships.

"When did Ben become convinced about his putting system, if ever?" I asked.

"After Jack Nicklaus won the last of 18 record major championships, the 1986 Masters tournament, putting his heart out at Augusta National, exactly as Ben had done in 1967, including matching Hogan's final nine hole score of 30," explained Wind.

Amazed by the nearly 20-year gap between 1967 and 1986, I understood that Hogan, the ultimate perfectionist, wanted to get things right for the good of the game. According to Wind, Hogan believed that

while Nicklaus's personal putting technique was not purely Hogan-esque, it was close enough for him to consider Jack a personal model and sort of ambassador for his system, and thus made him feel good about what he believed worked. Of course, Hogan's tournament record matters most in weighing the strength of his innovative four-stroke putting system.

Seeing Jack Nicklaus become so successful following essentially the same principles Hogan's own putting system was built around gave Hogan the confidence to realize he had truly cracked the code wide open and had something worth sharing with golfers of all handicaps.

In the lessons that follow, on behalf of Ben Hogan and his legacy, and for the good of the game, all the putting tenets of his four-stroke system are to be revealed, through my analysis along with those of other golf experts, including Herbert Warren Wind, who, when in Hogan's company, thankfully was never afraid to ask questions, clearing up once and for all the putting mystique surrounding this great champion.

CHAPTER 2
THE PROCESS

Ben Hogan discovered that the secret to developing exceptional putting skill and full control on any golf course's greens is to replace the power mind-set with a precision mind-set.

Ben Hogan's victory in The Open Championship of 1953, the third straight major championship he won, epitomized poetic justice as dished out by the Gods of Golf. Only 4 years earlier, in February 1949, Hogan was nearly killed in a car crash. Now he stood before thousands of fans, crowned "The Champion Golfer of the Year" by the captain of The Royal and Ancient Golf Club of St. Andrews. So historic was this victory at Carnoustie in Scotland, highlighted by a record final round, that Hogan's life story, with all its ups and downs, was documented in the film *Follow the Sun* and more recently in the wonderful biographical works by Curt Sampson, James Dodson, and David Barrett.

What has not been documented, up until now, is how Ben Hogan devised in his head a four-stroke system of putting, based on common sense and some scientific principles, while recuperating from the accident. Then later, once physically able to putt, he started testing out his methods and philosophy on the practice green first, and on the course second, and he knew right away that he was on to something big.

For the same reason that a golfer logically chooses a particular club for the distance at hand, say a 5-iron from 180 yards out, and logically employs four different techniques for hitting four different 180-yard shots to deal with four different lies or course situations, a player confronted with different putting situations on the greens during a round of golf must depend, logically, on employing different techniques as well. One golf swing, as you know, won't cut it. One type of putting stroke, as Ben Hogan wanted us to know, won't cut it either, yet the four strokes in the putting system Hogan invented will for sure. And according to Herbert Warren Wind, this is what this great champion intended to write about in the never-published *Five Lessons: The Modern Fundamentals of Putting.*

What sets Ben Hogan apart from all the golf coaches and experts who teach putting is that he incorporated four separate, distinctly different strokes into his putting arsenal, while at the same time adding his own nuances to each, as every other golfer reading this book should do to personalize his or her system. When Ben meditated on the swing and the putting game while recuperating from his car crash, he figured he would never play the game again on the professional stage. So what he was devising were systems for swinging and putting that the average golfer could benefit from.

No other golfer had ever won, in a single year, the Masters, the United States Open, and The Open Championship. Hogan's wins in 1953 proved he had devised a fault-free system for swinging a golf club and hitting all kinds of tee-to-green shots, most notably a super-controlled power-fade off the tee that starts left of target on a low trajectory, rises high fast, then slowly "fades" right toward a specific area of grass in the fairway, providing the best angle into the hole when hitting an approach shot. He also, not so incidentally, developed a system for sinking putts of varying distances on varying putting surfaces.

Hogan was a 9-year-old child when he witnessed his father, a blacksmith, commit suicide. That may explain to a degree why he became such a solitary golfer, a player known to withdraw to the end of the driving range to hit practice shots and to visit the putting green in the late afternoon or early evening to privately ingrain into his muscle memory what worked, to experiment further to find a new physical or mental link to better putting, all in an attempt to discover something special that he was in full control of—something that he promised to cherish and care for and that he would do everything in his power to hold onto forever, to never lose. Ben Hogan achieved all the goals he set out to accomplish, yet because he was not absolutely sure, by his perfectionist standards, that the methods he invented would work for all golfers, and because he felt better holding onto his putting secrets for fear of loss, he found it difficult to fully let go, delaying indefinitely work on *Five Lessons: The Modern Fundamentals of Putting*. Fortunately, enough information about Hogan's four-stroke putting method has been revealed, thanks to the clues he left us.

DURING A major championship, Hogan had a reputation for entering into a trancelike state right from the start of the tournament, only breaking the silence on the first tee by nodding to a fellow competitor or saying "good luck." Once it was Hogan's turn to tee off and hit the opening shot of the round, he spent extra time standing behind the ball and looking down the fairway until he picked out the ideal landing area and visualized the ball flying toward that ideal target, then landing on the grass and rolling on to Position A.

Next, standing to the side of the ball, he took more practice swings, sometimes closing his eyes to go deeper into himself and to feel the ideal swing action he wanted to repeat, since a good start to the round, in the form of a well-placed, powerfully hit drive, helped establish a strong base for him to feed off for the entire round.

Over the ball, on a tee shot, Hogan concentrated on feeling bounce in his feet, similar to the baseball shortstop standing in the ready position. Looking back and forth, from target to ball, Hogan would trigger the backswing and arrive at the top of the swing readied to shift and rotate his hips with a clearing action, opening a clear passageway for the club to come into the ball powerfully.

Out on the fairways, where the other shots are played, Hogan was all business, too: inside himself in his own world, strategizing, thinking about the upcoming shot even before reaching his tee shot and setting up to the ball to play an approach into the green. Hogan played in silence, as if kneeling down in church praying, only speaking to say "good shot" if the shot of a fellow player he was paired with was truly good by his strict standard.

Once reaching the first green, if facing a short or medium-length putt for birdie or to save par, or needing to hit a long lag putt up close to the hole, Hogan took extra time, concentrating on feeling the proper stroke technique through his hands and then executing the action, whichever of the four strokes from his system he chose for the particular situation on the green, knowing that holing a putt would signal to the psyche that he was in full control.

More than Harry Vardon, Bob Jones, Gary Player, Jack Nicklaus, or Nick Faldo

Ben Hogan may have missed Claude Harmon's ace in 1947 and gone winless that same year, yet he still had a winner at his side: Valerie Hogan, his wife and greatest fan, whom he lovingly called his "15th club."

(and particularly during a major championship), Ben Hogan had a reputation for being the ultimate grinder. Paying attention to planning or playing the shot the course situation dictated, on or off the green, Hogan was like a man possessed, even to the point of walking to his ball like a soldier on the march.

An incident that occurred at the 1947 Masters epitomizes this great player's ability to shut out the world and remain, for the entire round, in a mental cocoon. Hogan's playing partner, Claude Harmon, remarkably scored a hole-in-one on the par-three 12th hole, one of the toughest par-three holes in all of golf. Hogan, after Harmon picked the ball out of the hole, sank his putt for a birdie two.

As the story goes, both Claude and Ben walked to the 13th tee, hit their drives on the dogleg par-five, and walked down the fairway. Then, as Harmon was just starting to get ready to play his next shot, Hogan walked over to him and said, "You know, Claude, that's the first birdie I ever made on number 12," stunning Harmon, who thought Hogan was going to finally congratulate him for making an ace. Fortunately, Harmon believed Hogan was simply joking and brushed the situation off, pretending to ignore what was said.

Hogan was serious, however. All he had seen was the tee shot he hit fly high and land 12 feet from the hole, and the putt he stroked firmly into the cup for a birdie two. Believe it or not, Hogan really never saw Claude score the hole-in-one, nor did he hear the roar of the crowd. In his intense personal focus, he had blocked it out. Hogan was all alone in a singular battle with the golf course, and that was all he cared about, knowing that only by being 100% into his golf game could he win that battle and, as a result, beat everyone else in the field.

I realize that Ben Hogan's ability to block everything out is partly a God-given gift, partly the result of enduring traumatic personal tragedies, and partly developed through practice. But we do not have to be psychoanalytical about this or go back in time and get a full historical record to glean insight from his example. Rather, all that matters is that you realize how vitally important it is for you and every other golfer, pro or amateur, to put yourself in the right mind-set when playing golf, since this is one way you can cut strokes off your score without changing your swing. Furthermore, only by honing your mental game will you be able to putt to the best of your ability.

"Putting, it seems to me, is a matter of concentration, relaxation, and confidence," Hogan wrote in the chapter on putting in his book *Power Golf*. "Thus the mental phase of this department of the game looms at least as important as the physical phase, the action of stroking the ball into the hole, because mental strain while putting is probably responsible for more missed strokes than any other mistake in the physical mechanics of putting."

From working for *GOLF Magazine* and being privy to subscriber surveys and inside information provided by focus groups, and having conducted my own research, I can tell you with absolute certainty that the average golfer wants to improve the mental side of his or her game, yet just does not know how to go about it. The good news is, Hogan was the same way. But Ben realized that it wasn't necessary to earn degrees in psychiatry or psychology to understand how the mind can be used to improve one's putting scores. You can do the same thing. All you have to do is follow the examples set by Ben Hogan and his tips for using one's head to putt better.

When I first started investigating this side of Hogan's golf game, I went in search of all his mentors, thinking I would find some shrink somewhere in Texas or in a faraway land who helped him, kind of like when I found out when conducting research for a book on Tiger Woods that he had spent a lot of time with Dr. Jay Brunza, and that Earl Woods, Tiger's father, said his son's short game had really improved after seeing the doctor.

In Hogan's case, I found no record of a psychiatrist, psychologist, or certified social worker who helped him overcome the mental and/or emotional obstacles he faced on the course and in life. The reason I drew a blank was because Hogan himself was that man. He placed his faith in God, sure, but he prayed only for the will, knowing if he just was given that, he could win again. He got his wish by relying on himself and summoning the strength he needed from his Lord, who provided the strength Hogan found within himself.

Ninety-nine percent of golfers believe they have to putt great to gain confidence on the course. But you'll learn, as I learned, that confidence is a state of mind that you can conjure up by being spiritual and believing in God or by relying on a friend or family member to boost one's spirit and sense of self. So, whether you follow in Hogan's footsteps and walk with the Lord or go another route, go to the golf course convinced it is going to be a good day on the greens and that you will make a good stroke on every putt, rather than sink every putt. That way, you lower your expectations, so just in case you miss, you have a psychological out that involves a mental trick Jack Nicklaus used his entire career. Knowing you employed a good putting stroke, you simply convince yourself that you did not miss—the ball missed. This mind game is a parallel to the one 1992 Masters champion Fred Couples told me he uses, particularly in major championships. Fred putts with a carefree attitude; if the ball goes in, fine. If not, that's fine, too. And you see how this has helped Fred putt better, as he did in 2012 when he won the Senior British Open Championship.

Until you get deeper into the mental side of golf and find your way to conjure up confidence and to concentrate more intently, be sure to work hard on emulating Hogan's pre-stroke routine by following a step-by-step system for setting up to putt and visualizing

the perfect putt rolling along the correct line to the hole—a line you picked out when analyzing the green's contour, figuring out the direction and degree of break in the putting surface, or determining that you faced a straight putt.

It's important to stay positive too, as Hogan did, no matter what the state of the match, where you stand in the tournament, or the state of your game on that day. No matter how difficult the putt, never think about the magnitude of the putt's importance either, or what you don't want to do, such as picking your head up or taking your eye off the ball. Never focus on the negative, as negativity breeds fear. If you fear hitting the putt past the hole from long range, since it could roll off the green into a deep bunker, the putt you hit will likely finish up several feet, if not yards, short of the hole.

While conceding that Ben Hogan was a reclusive person who was difficult to figure out, sometimes I'm even more baffled by the occasional negative comments made over the years about Hogan's putting skills, especially since these off-putting, inaccurate statements are usually made by a prominent person in the golf business. Considering Hogan finished up his professional career winning 63 regular PGA Tour events and 9 major championships, all played over the most challenging golf courses featuring the trickiest greens designed to test the talent and nerve of the game's best players, I cannot—and I'm certain I never will—understand how Peter Alliss, the veteran golf professional, golf writer, and golf commentator for ABC/BBC television and Golf Channel, could have written in his book, 1983's *The Who's Who of Golf*, that "the prime cause of Hogan's decline was putting. Before his car crash, he was reckoned one of the best putters on the U.S. Tour. Thereafter, his putter was rarely a saver."

What makes this comment even more absurd is that after the accident, Ben Hogan won six major championships. Thankfully for posterity's sake, there are fewer negative quotes than positive quotes about Hogan's putting and none as absurd as the aforementioned that allegedly came from a man who could have made millions playing tournament golf had he been able to putt to pro standard. The fact is, this was not the case, as his license plate—"3-PUTT"—verifies. Yes, this is funny, but what he or Michael Hobbs, the book's researcher, said about Hogan is not one bit funny, nor is it a true statement.

Yes, it's true that Hogan missed a short putt

> It's important to stay positive, as Hogan did, no matter the state of the match, where you stand in the tournament, or the state of your game on that day.

in the 1956 U.S. Open that could have earned him a chance to win a fifth title, and yes, he told the press afterward that his nerves were shot. But there's another side to this story that I didn't learn about until 1987. At that time, Oscar Fraley, the former editor of *GOLF Magazine* and *Senior Golfer* and, most important, a friend of Ben Hogan's, told me that prior to the 1956 U.S. Open, Hogan did something so out of character that few knew about but that Hogan privately admitted cost him the title: He switched putters.

"Ben replaced the old reliable brass putter, with kind of a bull's-eye head design—the one that helped him win many tournaments and championships—for a lighter blade putter that he looked at, insisted he liked, and put it in his bag!" Fraley told me. "As you know, John, there's nothing wrong with switching putters, since this strategy of playing with a different putting club can spark a new sense of confidence that every golfer needs on the greens. The thing is, the lie angle of the new putter was too flat—really flat—which promoted an inside-inside stroke path that's okay for long putts but, as you know, spells

Ben Hogan's eye was so keen that he spotted something in Sam Snead's putting stroke that indicated Sam was playing with a club that was not suited to his natural setup and stroke. Look closely and you'll notice that on this short putt Sam swings the putter back along an inside path, then has to pull the club on-line in the hitting area, such that it makes square contact with the ball.

disaster on short putts, since it prevents the golfer, as it did Hogan, from employing an on-line square-to-square putting stroke.

"Worse still, because Hogan's stance was narrow on short putts and the back-stroke shorter, as was the tempo of the stroke, he actually swung the putter on an in-to-out path, with the putter's face failing to square up to the ball at impact, thereby causing the ball to be pushed out to the right of the hole. So it is no wonder Ben missed that putt. But the fact is he missed one short putt per round for the first three rounds that I bet you never heard about. Let me tell you, I don't get it. I could not believe Hogan would do such a thing, and it was really hard to watch."

Fraley's comments surprised me, because Hogan was known to be such a stickler for customized putters. He once even advised Sam Snead, his rival, that Sam's putter sat at the wrong lie angle and that he was letting the putter dictate the type of stroke employed, instead of the putter complementing the stroke, thus requiring Sam to manipulate the putter to return it squarely to the ball, which works only some of the time.

As I then searched for a reason Hogan would do such a foolish thing, I felt comfort in knowing that the great Hogan was human and capable of making mistakes. This one, however, made about as much sense as the guy who starts feeling age set in, dumps his

faithful wife of 40 years, and gets hooked up in a very serious way with a young woman, thinking he's in love when he's really in lust. You can probably guess what happened next. Yes, Hogan's putter, like the older wife, was returned to its rightful place. Both, after all, represented a custom fit.

What's fascinating about this story is how you can look inside the head of Ben Hogan and gain something that can save you strokes on the golf course. Hogan made an amateurish error by playing with a new putter that he believed would boost his confidence and allow him to putt better in a championship he was hoping to win. There's nothing wrong with that, since new putters can really work wonders, as long as they're suited to one's natural setup and stroke tendencies—in short, the bespoke putter. If the putter is not customized, it is like wearing a size 9 shoe instead of the size 11 you normally wear.

WHAT'S SO special about Ben Hogan's golf game, as we continue studying it, is that Ben brought a new aspect to golf that applied to every single shot he hit, whether played with a driver, fairway club, middle-iron, wedge, or putter, and that was control.

"When you watched Ben Hogan swing and hit drives on the practice range, to a caddie some 275 yards out, waiting for each ball to land, the caddie would never move off his spot; just reach out his left arm or right arm, step forward a couple of feet or move a couple of feet back. Now that's control," said Ken Venturi, a great player and friend of Hogan's. "Out on the course, Hogan was so accurate that he'd hit the flagstick with iron shots, and not just once every few tournaments, pretty much an average of one time per round, and on the greens when he got hot he was so deadly with the putter you'd swear he became a machine overnight. Now that's control."

Venturi really hits the mark here, and that's because he knew Hogan's game. When I asked him if Hogan was in full control of his putter, he proved what a keen observer he is.

"John," he said, "we all have great days on the golf course, and we all have really bad days. What I'm trying to say is that overall, yes, Ben was in full control. And sure, he'd miss a putt here and there. All players, even the greatest, do. Ben was a great player who holed a lot of money putts during his career—critical putts in major championships. As good as Ben was with the driver and irons, you must remember that those clubs are hit into the air. On the greens, you can sometimes hit the perfect putt, and because of a tiny imperfection, a high spot that the mower missed, a barely visible peb-

ble, the smallest of spike scars . . . whatever. My point: Greens are not billiard tables. I'll leave you to fill in the blanks."

Venturi certainly hits the mark here, too, as only he can, when describing Ben Hogan's ability to control all shots. However, when taking the element of control to a higher level, no one ever described this aspect of Hogan's game better than the late Bert Randolph Sugar. I sat down and spoke with Sugar at the Creek Club on Long Island during the Wall Street Charity Classic, when he gave me a signed copy of his book *The 100 Greatest Athletes of All Time*, in which Ben Hogan was profiled.

"Playing with precision that bordered on complete control—almost to the point where he could control every one of the 336 dimples on the golf ball—Hogan imposed his iron will on opponent and course alike, and on himself as well, willing his own comeback and greatness," Sugar said.

MILLIONS OF golfers who have read and continue to read *Five Lessons: The Modern Fundamentals of Golf* know that Ben Hogan unraveled the mystery of the golf swing and pushed forward through days and months and years of frustration to perfect the power-fade technique for hitting super-controlled shots. However, a very small percentage of golfers, infinitesimal really, know that Hogan's career victories would not be in the record books forever had it not been for the Texas-born golf star's putting prowess, a talent he had to work at, starting in 1932, a year after turning pro, when he met tour professional Henry Picard.

Back then, Picard and Hogan were discussing putting one summer evening at the Glen Garden Club, when Picard commented that all leading putters on tour putted differently. This one comment was construed by most to simply mean everyone has his own personalized stroke. Hogan took it another way, however, concluding that more than one sound stroke was needed to sink a variety of putts on level or sloped greens, fast, medium-pace, or slow putting surfaces covered in bent grass, Bermuda grass, or, less often, poa annua grass.

Said another way: Each course situation, on or off the green, that the golfer confronts demands its own strategy and technical solution. Now all Ben needed to do was go out and prove his theory, by going through The Process. But unlike all great players before him, who looked to figure out one aspect of the swing or shot-making game, Hogan wanted to invent a whole new system of putting, not just one aspect of the putting stroke.

Hogan set off on a new journey that involved analyzing the pros who were the best short-range, medium-range, and long-range putters on slow and fast greens, with the idea of finding one model in each category. In addition, Hogan began studying all aspects of the putting game and experimenting with various nuances in order to personalize his own basic setup and stroke positions. It would take him years to perfect his new and improved four-stroke system and decades for him to be 100% sure that it would work for all golfers.

> Each course situation, on or off the green, that the golfer confronts demands its own strategy and technical solution.

Hogan sank a bunch of birdie putts in both the 1946 and 1948 PGA Championships, contested then by the hole-by-hole match play format, and won both times by big margins. But regardless of how well Hogan putted in all nine major championships he won, this most vital part of his golf game that he was learning to master was ignored by television golf analysts, sportscasters, golf writers, and the like, simply because they had never seen any pro golfer hit so many consistent power-fade shots and soft fades into greens.

Furthermore, prioritizing by the golf industry, even back then, to recognize power over putting, chiefly via advertisements designed to lure country club golfers into pro shops across America to try to buy a power game by spending money on driving equipment when, instead, the majority of golfers should be spending extra money on custom-fit putters designed to help them putt more proficiently on the greens, caused golf's ground game to take a backseat. Putting was rarely talked about, causing Hogan to do some rethinking regarding his desire to write a book on putting fundamentals, figuring the timing was bad, and figuring right. The mistake Ben made, in my mind, was to look at the situation solely from a commercial point of view rather than considering what should be done for the good of the game. I shared my thoughts on this with Wind, who defended Hogan, telling me that it was no use for Ben to go through the effort of writing his magnum opus on putting if the majority of country club golfers only cared about hitting drives a long way off the tee.

I conceded that Mr. Wind was right. It was difficult to reach America's golf audience, composed mainly of wealthy men belonging to expensive private clubs and possessed of a Babe Ruth mentality in which they confused the objective of golf—low scoring—with the object of America's apple pie sport of baseball: to slug the ball over the center-field fence and out of the park.

To make matters worse, more articles in golf magazines were written in those days on the subject of long hitting than on the secrets to sinking putts. Furthermore, as more golf magazines entered the marketplace, more advertisements for the latest power golf equipment were appearing in these popular publications and, later, on television. Without fail, these features and ads always involved a brand-new club feature, such as a springy shaft that would "kick" and "release" the club head faster into impact and, in turn, catapult the ball far down the fairway, together with a brand-new hot golf ball produced by a leading golf company.

What I call "power pushers"—teaching professionals, tour pros, celebrity spokespersons, and chief operating officers of major golf companies—overwhelmed golfers in the 1950s, and even more so in the '60s, '70s, '80s, and '90s. They had anxious golfers making frequent visits to the ever-growing number of golf discount shops around the country to test out a variety of drivers by hitting balls into a net (while watching a favorite golfer appear on a big screen selling distance), then 5 minutes later slapping big bucks down on the counter and walking out of the store with a hot driver and a dozen hot golf balls, hoping and praying they had just bought a new and improved driving game, as seen on TV!

There's no doubt that PGA Tour sluggers in Ben Hogan's time and John Daly's time make for exciting television, help the TV ratings, bring in the big galleries, allow the PGA Tour to donate millions of dollars to charitable causes, and stimulate growth among junior golfers, our next generation of players. But what has hurt the game are power pushers who give country club golfers the impression that golf's power game, highlighted by long driving, is more important than its precision game, including putting.

Please don't misunderstand the instructional message being relayed here. Power off the tee is every golfer's obsession, which makes sense to a certain degree. After all, the longer the golfer can drive the ball, the shorter the iron left to the green on a par-four hole, which increases the player's chances of hitting an iron approach shot to within birdie range of the hole. Granted, too, a powerful drive on a par-five increases the player's chance of reaching the green in two shots, rather than the regulation three shots on this type of hole, and sets up an eagle or birdie opportunity. Furthermore, in match play competitions, the golfer who can boom the ball off the tee, well past an opponent's ball lying in the fairway, carries a huge psychological advantage over his or her opponent. The irony is that the longer hitter does not always win the match or shoot the lowest score in a stroke play tournament, even if

that same player hits powerful tee shots straight down the center of the "short grass"—a lesson Ben Hogan learned the hard way.

Controlled power is a good thing, but there's no escaping one golfing fact: In order to shoot low scores consistently, as Ben Hogan did during the 1950s, golfers must be able to sink putts of varying lengths and putt well on sloping greens, on super-fast or super-slow surfaces, and on greens with different type grasses. While I realize that the golfer's obsession with power has about as much chance of going away totally as lobbyists leaving Washington, I'd like all golfers to realize what Ben Hogan and other professionals from the past and present realize: Power is of no true value unless you can combine it with accuracy. What's more, putting is still more important to shooting low scores, so much so that what was said long ago remains true: "Drive for show, putt for dough."

What's disappointing about the status quo of golf in America is that surveys conducted by *GOLF Magazine* over the past 30 years have shown virtually no improvement in golfers' handicaps, regardless of the billions of dollars spent by millions of golfers on fancy new drivers and golf balls.

At last, average country club golfers are finding out what the full scope of the golf media has gotten wrong about the world's greatest golfers, owing to an obsession with power golf. In short, a new, expensive driver is not the answer to shooting lower scores, regardless of what you see in television or print advertisements. Furthermore, no matter how good a player's swing or shot-making game, if he or she cannot sink a high percentage of putts, at the end of the round or tournament that same player will fail to win the club championship at their home club or, in the case of a tour player, fail to bring home the winner's check.

The chief reason great golfers such as Harry Vardon, Bob Jones, Walter Hagen, Arnold Palmer, Jack Nicklaus, Tom Watson, Lee Trevino, and Phil Mickelson all came to dominate the field in major championships and to stay in the spotlight long enough during their careers to be inducted into golf's Hall of Fame has to do with an ability to hit solid drives down the fairway and controlled iron shots onto the green, to think strategically, and to hit good recovery shots after a bad shot or bad bounce leaves their ball in what British golf commentators typically refer to as a "spot of bother." But most of all, the most critical component of their success is an ability to sink putts under the pressure of stiff competition, particularly down the stretch, on the world stage, with everything at stake.

Interviews I've conducted with average golfers indicate that many still three-putt several holes per round and miss a high number of short and medium-length putts, even though putting equipment has improved greatly and PGA-affiliated golf pros are better informed now than they were in days gone by about the effects of club design on the putting stroke and roll of the ball, in terms of distance and direction control. The problem I see getting worse is that there is an increasing number of non-PGA-affiliated pros teaching golf who should never be allowed to give instruction. They lack the proper training and the years of experience a PGA professional gets while serving as an apprentice, then an assistant professional, and attending all of the seminars, putting in the necessary time to become properly accredited as a Class A golf professional. In addition, so much emphasis has been placed on the swing that I have to revert to what Claude Harmon taught his son, Butch, about his method of teaching. "I don't teach swing," the elder Harmon said. "I teach golf."

Speaking of teaching, Ben Hogan learned some valuable putting lessons from Claude Harmon. One of the most important relates to the address position, as per the instructional message in the caption of the classic Masters photograph on page 43.

Think about those words, just for a second, and you'll realize how important putting is to playing golf. There are no exceptions to

Here we see Hogan closely watching friend and fellow competitor Claude Harmon, when they were playing together in the 1950 Masters. This experience would prove valuable to Hogan, who noticed that Harmon crouched over like he did when setting up, but with less bend at the knees, and seemed to make a smoother-looking stroke that was very effective. In setting up with less bend, Hogan's shoulders, arms, hands, and wrists suddenly relaxed—a sure link to employing a more even-tempo stroke.

Bobby Locke's inside putting stroke (above, left) was so ideal for long putts on slow greens that Ben Hogan incorporated elements of it into his own putting system. On the other hand, Locke's inside-to-inside stroke does not work well on short putts, since the hook-spin imparted on the ball at impact can cause the ball to spin out of the cup (above, right).

the rule, either. Even Tiger Woods, if he is to rise to the top again by winning major championships, will need to sink putts, again and again and again. And to accomplish this goal, Tiger will also have to do what Nicklaus did after not winning a major championship for 6 years and what Hogan did after recovering from his car crash, which is precisely the same as every other PGA Tour, LPGA Tour, Champions Tour, and Nationwide Tour player has had to do when making a comeback: Study the method of a great putter, ideally Ben Hogan, and adopt one or more of his setup and stroke positions, which is what Jack Nicklaus did. Then add your own nuances to personalize your stroke.

Buy a putter with a look and feel that trigger a new sense of confidence, then seek out a local pro or club maker to be sure your "flat stick" is perfectly suited to your natural, comfortably correct setup position and innate stroke tendencies. When checking that the putter is a perfect fit for you, pay particular attention to the club's loft, grip size, lie, and shaft flex.

When hitting a long putt on a very slow green, Hogan would swing the putter on a shallower path, then rotate his right hand slowly over his left through the hitting area, closing the club face at impact and imparting hook-spin on the ball, in a very similar fashion to Bobby Locke, the South African who Hogan claimed was the best putter ever. Locke's method, with the resulting spin it produces, allows the ball to roll all the way to the hole, so you don't have to be concerned with employing a longer or faster back-stroke action. Many golf experts I interviewed agreed that this method of Locke's is a high percentage play on long putts, but a low percentage play on short putts.

When Locke used this flat stroke on short putts, the ball struck with exaggerated over-spin tended to spin out of the cup after doing a 360, as in 360 degrees in a circle, and ended up on the edge of the cup or several feet away, depending whether the greens were covered in Bermuda grass that slows the roll or bent grass that speeds up the roll. This fault cost Locke a couple of major championships. Phil Mickelson stopped employing

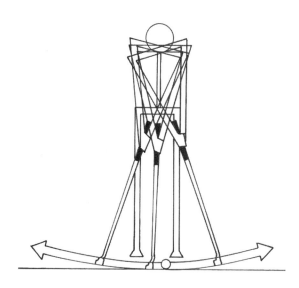

This square-to-square stroke, ideal for hitting short and medium-length putts on super-fast greens, was favored by Ben Hogan and, today, is advocated by putting guru Dave Pelz. While Pelz demands the golfer position his or her arms directly underneath the sockets of the shoulders to employ a square-to-square putting action, Hogan's secret to a square robotic stroke is positioning his eyes directly over the target line, slightly behind the ball.

a similar flat-putting action, as advocated by Stan Utley, and instead returned to the straight back-straight through stroke advocated by Dave Pelz, after missing a few critical short putts down the stretch at the 2004 U.S. Open at Shinnecock Hills.

You'll sink more short putts, too, if you employ a square stroke, as long as you make sure the putter moves through the ball instead of moving up, which is a mistake I have seen many aspiring players make. This fault usually can be attributed to controlling the straight back-straight through stroke by rocking the shoulders in an exaggerated fashion during the start-to-finish action. When you come into impact as described, with the putter moving up, you add too much loft to the putter, promoting an uneven roll of the ball and a putt that tends to fall short of the hole.

The player who plays the ball too far forward in the stance or dips the right shoulder dramatically at the start of the down-stroke is the one who will send the putter up, rather than keeping it moving low and along the target line in a streamlined fashion, before and just after impact.

Golf is a game of inches. On the greens, it's a game of fractions of inches. This is why I believe you will benefit greatly from Hogan's four-stroke putting system as well as all of the other elements vital to the process involved in improving one's putting skills. As Hogan proved, this process can make the difference between a putted ball falling into the cup or hanging on the lip of the hole.

Every element of the process is vital. In the case of the setup, for short putts on fast greens, grip pressure is an important factor. Hogan held the club firmly on short putts to keep the putter's face square to the target on the back-stroke and down-stroke. However, because Ben found that he sometimes

gripped the putter's handle so firmly he lost all feel, he found security in a new grip, which you can see pictured on the cover of this book.

Grip pressure, though vitally important, is only one part of an overall process that demands the same degree of patience and perseverance and diligent practice that Hogan worked through to accomplish his end goal of developing a new way of swinging. The next step in the process is to physically rehearse the address position (setup) then each back-and-through stroke action. At this point, conscious thought still plays an important role in the process, and it will continue to do so until every position and movement has been drilled into your muscle memory. When this goal is accomplished, and your mind trusts that your body will operate according to its job description, your conscious mind will step out of your way. This, in simple terms, is what is meant by letting go. One can only let go completely when all of the individual movements of one's putting stroke can be employed without thinking consciously about each, and they flow together naturally as one. Through practice, you, like Ben Hogan before you, will be able to set up to the ball and then let go as the subconscious mind and muscle memory control the stroke. That is a good feeling and one Hogan told his personal assistant Greg Hood is a sure sign of good results to come on the putting green.

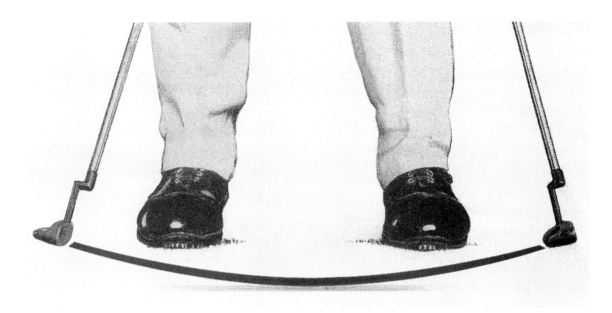

The larger illustration shows a close-up view of the club moving on a square path along the target line, but to the trained eye something looks wrong. As indicated by the smaller illustration, the putter rises up at impact, causing the effective loft of the putter to be increased dramatically, thereby producing a ball that bounces when it leaves the putter's face and falls short of the hole, rather than starting its smooth roll over the putting surface immediately after impact.

Every golfer out there, pro and amateur alike, would be pleased to put their putting game on automatic pilot, as Hogan did for much of his career to such great effect. Why Hogan's methodology stands in such stark contrast to other anachronistic putting techniques is because he managed to bring together the elements of a custom-fit putter and matched them up with various techniques. For example, instead of having to be concerned that his hands were slightly ahead of the ball at address and through the impact area, so that the roll of the ball would be pure, he made sure the loft in his putter was reduced. Hogan actually considered carrying two bespoke putters in the bag, one upright to be used for short and medium putts, the other flat for long putts, and I believe you'll see more and more players carry two putters in the decades ahead. The reason is, as I have mentioned already, that short and medium-length putts call for the putter to swing on a straight path, while longer putts demand the golfer swing the putter along a slightly curved path.

It is important to note, again, that Hogan tailored each putting stroke to the specific situation at hand. When facing a short or medium-length putt on a fast-rolling bent grass green, he employed a square putting action reminiscent of Jack Burke Jr.'s during his heyday of the 1950s. And when facing a long putt on a slow Bermuda grass green, Hogan employed a hybrid form of Bobby Locke's inside-stroke, calling for a slight degree of right-to-left sidespin to be imparted on the golf ball.

Why doesn't Hogan's system include the inside-square-inside putting stroke advocated by short game guru Stan Utley for all putts, or incorporate the putting philosophy advocated by putting expert Dave Pelz that the golfer should hit all putts hard enough to reach an imaginary cup 17 inches behind the hole? For starters, employing Utley's inside-square-inside stroke requires a precise timing, which means hours and hours of practice time is required—too much time for the average amateur. Besides, this type of action imparts such a high degree of hot sidespin on the ball that unless the ball enters the cup dead-center, it will inevitably spin out off one of its sides and end up several feet past the cup, especially from short range.

As for the ideal speed of a putt, suffice it to say that overall the die putter will make more putts than the charge-the-hole putter.

As for the ideal speed of a putt, suffice it to say that overall the die putter will make more putts than the charge-the-hole putter. Furthermore, I can never imagine myself trying to hit a putt on the slowest of greens 17 inches past an imaginary hole, let alone on low-cut greens that read high on the Stimpmeter.[1] By God, if you followed that advice at a course like Augusta National, Winged Foot, Shinnecock Hills, or any other

---

1 As defined by the editors of *GOLF Magazine*, a Stimpmeter, in the simplest definition, is a bar 3 feet in length and made of aluminum. It has a V-shaped groove running down the center and a notch 6 inches from one end, in which the ball rests. Invented by Edward Stimpson, a low-handicap golfer, as a way to bring uniform speed to greens, the "meter" is placed on a flat area of the green and raised up to about a 20-degree angle, such that the ball leaves its notch, then rolls down the slope onto the green. The distance the ball travels represents the "stimp" reading. So, should the ball roll 12 feet before coming to rest, 12 is the speed of the green and considered fast.

venue with super-speedy putting surfaces, the ball would finish in another county.

Hogan was critical of unorthodox strokes like those advocated by Utley. Back-and-through actions are difficult to repeat consistently due to the numerous moving parts involved that require perfect timing to work well, and Hogan knew that the fewer moving parts a stroke requires, the easier it is to repeat. The unorthodox putting methods of today do work well at times, yet they require a tremendous amount of eye-hand coordination and such a heightened degree of feel for the positions of the swinging putter that average golfers as well as many tour professionals struggle to putt well consistently while employing them. Furthermore, each

method fails to hold up well under pressure, as evidenced by LPGA star Natalie Gulbis, who has not won a major championship while employing a split-handed putting stroke, even though she's a talented driver and iron player. The same goes for male players such as Sergio Garcia, who experimented with a claw grip and found it failed to work well enough for this superb tee-to-green player to win a major championship. The good news is Sergio finally got smart, going to a conventional putting grip that helped him stroke putts more solidly and accurately, win the 2012 Greensboro Open, and putt well in the 2012 Ryder Cup, contributing to Europe's victory over the United States.

By the time Byron Nelson (left) and Ben Hogan (right) returned to Glen Garden for an exhibition reunion match, on a very cold day in Fort Worth, Texas, Hogan had become the better putter. Hogan had learned so much about putting during the years following his loss to Nelson in Glen Garden's Caddie Championship in 1923. Hogan had made it a habit to practice on humid days, when feeling tired, on very cold days, in light rain—in any and all conditions one could expect to be confronted with on the golf course.

CHAPTER 3:
BEN HOGAN'S MAGIC GARDEN

Early putting lessons from top teachers and tour professionals at the Glen Garden Club in Fort Worth, Texas, helped Ben Hogan's skills on the green blossom.

"From every observation I have made of putting, there's no reason why the average player cannot putt reasonably well, since putting is merely rolling the ball over the surface of the green by striking it a gentle but firm blow. Yet, in spite of its apparent simplicity, many golfers who are capable of playing excellent golf from tee-to-green have difficulty when faced with the problem of getting the ball into the hole with a putter.

"Par on most courses allows 36 putting strokes per round, two on each hole. Therefore, it's worth your while to improve your putting because putting is the one department of the game in which most of us can cut down on the number of strokes by constant effort and practice. You can lose a stroke on the fairway and have a chance to make it up before completing the hole, but a stroke lost on the green is lost forever. This is why putting, while apparently simple, assumes such importance in the game."

If I were to poll a representative sample of the estimated 28 million golfers who play on public, private, semiprivate, resort, and municipal courses across America each year, asking each to attribute the preceding quote on putting and its importance to scoring to a professional golfer from a past or present era, chances are the names Bobby Locke, Billy Casper, Jack Nicklaus, Arnold Palmer, Tom Watson, Ben Crenshaw, Phil Mickelson, or Tiger Woods would form the likely short list of guesses submitted. Very few, if any, would ever mention Ben Hogan, who wrote those very words in his book *Power Golf*.

By the same token, if you asked even golf historians to pinpoint the key turning point in Ben Hogan's pro golf career, the answer would likely be one of the following:

> Experimental practice is something the greatest putters throughout history have done, from Walter Hagen to Seve Ballesteros to Tiger Woods.

1. The day in 1939 when Henry Picard told Hogan he would back him financially, if need be, so he could literally stay in the game until he found his comfort zone and started earning money from playing golf on tour.

2. Hogan's horrific head-on car crash with a Greyhound bus in 1949, which forced him to stop hitting hundreds of practice shots per day and instead start analyzing the swing and putting stroke from an intellectual perspective.

3. Hogan's return to the winner's circle for the first time since his accident, miraculously coming back to earn a victory in the 1950 U.S. Open at Merion.

4. Going three-for-three in the major championships of 1953, a feat that was unimaginable after the accident, when some doctors believed Hogan would never walk again.

No one except the late Herbert Warren Wind could have guessed that it was none of the above, but instead a seemingly insignificant event, losing the final of the Caddie Championship at the Glen Garden Club in Fort Worth, Texas, to Byron Nelson (even though young Ben was the better driver and approach shot player), that represented the true turning point in Hogan's life.

This loss, due mostly to some missed putts, was the best lesson in Hogan's golf career, because it made him realize that the art of scoring requires you to have full control over your complete game from tee to green and, not to be discounted, the ability to hit good putts consistently. Hogan's loss to Nelson taught the youngster to devote equal time to putting practice. Hogan did more, however, than spend hours and hours practicing putts. He became a putting scholar.

The more Hogan read up on putting or listened to the advice of others, however, the more he was led astray by misinformation. Fundamentals that were supposed to fit all golfers and promote a good putting stroke failed to work for him. Further, when Hogan would raise the subject of a custom-fit putter, veteran members at his home club, Glen Garden, would invariably say with a chuckle: "Good putters can sink putts with a broomstick."

Hogan had been around golf long enough to know going in that developing a consistent putting system was going to be extremely time-consuming and, frankly, a grind mentally, due to the inherent frustrations of trial and error. Yet he faced this challenge head-on, knowing that only by finding a foolproof method of putting could he play better and more consistently, and realize his dream of winning all four major championships. Ben knew this really meant discovering an entirely new system that would allow him—and all golfers—to sink putts of varying lengths on a variety of putting surfaces. This path was the only one he could take in order to evolve into a truly complete player, one in control of all aspects of the golf game. There was (and still is) no shortcut to that goal.

Hogan spent his early teenage years experimenting on the practice greens—moving the ball around in the stance, setting his hands in line, ahead, or slightly behind the ball at address, setting most of his body weight on the left foot, right foot, and balancing weight evenly, keeping his dominant eye over the golf ball, over the target line, and inside the target line, standing tall with arms hanging down outstretched and crouching with both arms bent at the elbows—in search of the best way to set up to the ball. Then he did the same type of experimenting with stroke actions.

One time, Hogan would swing the putter straight back along the target line and then straight through on the identical path. Another time, he would see how the ball reacted when he swung the putter along an inside-square-inside path. He experimented with impact positions, too; one time hitting the top portion of the ball, another time the middle of the ball, and other times the bottom half of the ball, always changing the tempo of the stroke from slow to medium to an upbeat tempo, all in an attempt to see which method allowed him to swing the putter the most rhythmically and to determine which technique worked best and in what specific situation on the green.

All of this experimental practice was a great idea, and it is something the greatest of short-game players and putters throughout history have done, from Walter Hagen to Seve Ballesteros to Tiger Woods, and in all cases there was always a coach or coaches, present or in the background, to guide and encourage the player to work on short shots and putting. In Ben Hogan's case, he was lucky to have been tutored by pro golfers who were connected directly to Glen Garden or were frequent visitors of the club, like club professional Ted Longworth and Henry Picard, who became Hogan's longtime mentor. Thankfully for Hogan's sake, both of these men were anything but by-the-book coaches.

Practicing this way really opened Hogan up to a new world of putting exploration, prompting the sometimes stubborn Texan to admit that golf's ground game wasn't so boring a component of the game after all. Searching for a new set of fundamentals, even unorthodox setup and stroke positions, Hogan started to realize what only the great putters throughout history realize: that putting is a multifaceted endeavor in which one's mind-set, sense of touch, tempo, timing, and rhythm all play vital roles. I hope, for the sake of your future as a putter, that you too realize what Hogan realized—namely, that the simple-looking act of rolling a golf ball, 1.68 inches in diameter, into a hole measuring $4^{1}/_{4}$ inches in diameter involves a lot of variables. Nevertheless, if you immerse yourself in experimental practice, then work on Hogan's unique practice drills that are described in this book's special insert, you will be well

Ben Hogan's instructional epiphany involved discovering an inarguable parallel between shot-making and putting. In short, just as four different lies on a golf course demand the golfer to employ four different techniques to hit a left-to-right fade shot (above), a right-to-left draw shot (right), a solid shot from a threadbare lie (page 56, left), and a recovery shot from a divot scar in the fairway (page 56, right), four different putting situations on the greens demand four different stroke techniques.

on your way to becoming an outstanding putter.

Hogan certainly put in the time. And between the ages of 19 and 31 he received a first-class education at what I consider to be Glen Garden University, a private golf school boasting an extremely talented faculty.

While I came to learn how Hogan was helped to become a better putter just by observing the Grout brothers, Dick and Jack, hit practice putts, making mental notes of what they did best and then experimenting with these elements in his own practice,

I was fascinated to learn how close he came as a teenager to discovering, on his own, an innovative putting system.

A friend of mine, Joseph Walker III, who worked with Byron Nelson on a golf diary in the mid-'90s, said that Nelson was told by Hogan that, in his search for the ideal stroke, Hogan found that one method worked better on short putts than long putts and another better on long putts than short putts. The thing is, neither Nelson nor Hogan thought much of this observation at the time. In fact, Hogan told Nelson he believed he was going backward instead of making progress, since he had always been taught to try to develop a singular, all-encompassing putting stroke. Hogan carried on, continuing to search for the one ideal stroke that in some ways set his progress back in a big way, because in the end he found that two main strokes and two hybrid offshoots of these strokes are what the golfer needs to succeed on the greens.

In spite of this, Hogan still learned a great deal about putting from the Glen Garden Club's circle of tour pros and teachers. By talking constantly about putting and testing out all kinds of setups and strokes, he began working, incrementally, toward the four-stroke system he eventually arrived at.

Ben Hogan turned professional in 1931, at the age of 19; becoming more mature by the day, he began working on mastering the game of golf. The moment Hogan started paying as much attention to putting as he did to the full swing, he came to the conclusion that there is a fine line between good driving skills and great driving skills, but an even finer line that separates the top putters.

Hogan's philosophical awakening did not happen until much later, though. First, he had to learn to appreciate what was so special about the good putting games of players like Ralph Guldahl, Craig Wood, Paul Runyan, Art Wall, and Doug Ford; the streaky putting games of Sam Snead and Jimmy Demaret; and the great putting games of

Jack Burke Jr., Henry Picard, Byron Nelson, Claude Harmon, and Bobby Locke. Then he had to figure out why some players were better short and medium-length putters than long putters, and vice versa.

As Hogan continued to mature as a player, he also realized that a golfer can miss a fairway by as much as 20 yards on a par-four or par-five hole and find oneself hitting off the short grass with a good angle into the green to hit an approach shot. But on the greens there is no such margin for error.

Whether missing the hole on a par-three, where putting makes up 66.6% of your total score, a par-four, where putting makes up 50% of your score, or a par-five, where two putts—considered regulation or par—make up 40% of your score, Hogan knew that the golfer who cannot putt with consistency pays a heavy price. The situation is even worse for pro golfers who depend on playing good golf to earn money to provide for their families. Furthermore, with fields full of excellent swingers and shot-makers, results almost always come down to the game played on the greens. Consequently, one miss or make per round can make the difference between winning or losing a tournament, particularly the major championships, which draw extraordinarily talented fields.

Facing up to the reality of golfing life, Ben decided to sacrifice playing time for practice time, and in his usual methodical way began his search not just for a better way to putt, but for the *best ways* to putt, knowing that, as on drives and approach shots, different shots with the same club require different techniques.

On his way to discovering the four-stroke putting system, Hogan collected and processed an incredible amount of data by observing the respective putting techniques employed by PGA-affiliated club professionals like Dick and Jack Grout and leading tour professionals like Henry Picard; studying photographs showing top-notch amateur golfers from the past, namely Walter Travis and Bob Jones; and learning from members of the Glen Garden Club who Ben caddied for on weekends during his youth and friends like Byron Nelson. All of those players had a knack for holing putts on different types of greens, and what he learned from experimenting with various elements of their techniques proved invaluable as he developed and refined his own technique.

Hogan felt strongly that the hand of God played a role in his development as a golfer, believing that even his accident was part of a divine plan for getting him to look at life

and golf differently and to develop a winning game.

"I play to win, and I think the Lord has let me win for a purpose," Ben Hogan wrote in a *Saturday Evening Post* article reflecting on his incredible 1953 season. "I hope that purpose is to give courage to those people who are sick or injured and broken in body."

Herbert Warren Wind supported this statement. "Ben told me that it was too much of a stretch to believe that by fate or chance alone so many golf experts would walk into his life at a golf course few had even heard of—the Glen Garden Club in Fort Worth, Texas," Wind said. "Ben believed God played a major role in leading him to men who would take him in like a son and train and treat him well."

Hogan had a point. Glen Garden was no Augusta National. But once Hogan committed himself to building a new putting system, several greats did come to help the youngster sort out the complexities of putting and make sense of all the hundreds of variables that come into play on a golf course's greens. Whether it was God's guiding light or the hand of fate that brought Hogan to "The

> One miss or make per round can make the difference between winning or losing a tournament, particularly the major championships.

Garden" and kept him coming back, he certainly met the right people there.

Dick Grout, the head professional at Glen Garden, chatted frequently with Hogan about golf equipment. In 1931, when Hogan turned pro, he would sometimes spend an hour or so with Dick, asking questions about putters. What he gained most from these chats was the knowledge that lie and loft are the most important features of a putter and that "it's not the putter, it's the puttee." This simply isn't true. Granted, a good putter can putt okay with any putter, but only by playing with a proven system, ideally Hogan's, and with a custom-fit putter can a golfer reach his or her potential as a putter and consistently sink a higher percentage of putts during a round of 18 holes. It was this groundwork that established the base from which Ben Hogan later became an expert on the intricate features of golf clubs in general (especially the driver, pitching wedge, and putter—what Jim McLean calls The Three Scoring Clubs), and what Hogan learned represent the guts of the game, even more so after meeting club maker Gene Sheeley.

Ben Hogan was so inquisitive about equipment that he constantly experimented, doing such things as adding lead tape to the back of the putter's head to see if the heavier weight enhanced his feel for the swinging putter when striking the ball

and, in turn, aided distance control. Hogan also tried both lengthening and shortening the steel shaft of his putter in order to determine how each change altered his putting action, for better or worse. He also painted a red dot on the top of the putter head, above where he had determined the sweet spot of the putter actually was located—off center, next to the club's neck—to see if this mark helped him line the putter's face up squarely to the ball and whether this was at the expense of the dot distracting him during the stroke. Hogan made the grip of the putter thinner, too, by removing one layer of double-sided tape under the grip, to determine if this helped promote a hand-wrist controlled stroke or instead encouraged exaggerated use of the hands and wrists, turning a potential positive into a negative. Hogan also tried thickening the grip by adding two extra layers of double-sided tape underneath it to see if this helped reduce any feeling of looseness between the hands and the putter's handle that could cause the putter to move off its intended stroke path during the back-and-through actions.

You can tell just from reading these few examples of Hogan's tinkering with the putter he carried most often in his bag when playing in a tournament (the one with the brass head made out of an old doorknob) that he had a passion for golf clubs and for getting

Hogan had become such a good putter, especially from short distance, that this photo taken during a practice round shows Ben's playing partner looking very intently at Hogan putting, trying to figure out his secret for sinking so many more putts than he did in previous years. It seemed, once the word got out among pro golf's technically minded players that Ben's putting game had reached a high standard, more and more of them showed a strong interest in playing a practice round with Hogan.

things right—or should we say perfect? Consequently, you will not be surprised to learn that he started his own Ben Hogan Golf Company. It will not surprise you either to find out that Hogan was a stickler for details regarding club manufacturing and club makeup, as confirmed by his former personal assistant Greg Hood and as did his personal club maker (and head club maker for Ben Hogan Golf), Gene Sheeley.

One chief reason Hogan showed such a strong interest in putting, starting around 1931 when he and Nelson returned to Glen Garden, was that he heard stories from Henry Picard about the tour's toughness and how you had to learn to get over the shock of shooting the best round you believed you could shoot and still get beaten by several shots, usually because the player atop the leaderboard sank more putts and thus fewer strokes to get around the course.

Jack Grout, a true student of the game, worked as assistant professional to his older brother Dick at Glen Garden from 1930 to 1937. Although Jack was to become the longtime teacher of Jack Nicklaus, starting around 1950 at Scioto Country Club in Columbus, Ohio, he gave Hogan some valuable putting tips. This is likely the very reason that, years later, when Nicklaus was to play with Hogan starting at the 1960 U.S. Open at Cherry Hills, Hogan noticed Nicklaus observing his putting techniques care-fully, looking for anything he may have missed or that Grout had failed to share with him.

During the "Grout years" at Glen Garden, in some respects, Hogan's putting progress was improving faster than were his skills with the driver. Hogan dedicated himself to improving his putting so much at this time that Olin Dutra, the 1934 U.S. Open champion, paid him a great compliment. "Ben wasn't good on the greens, but he made himself good," Dutra is quoted as saying in Greg Gregston's 1978 book, *Hogan: The Man Who Played for Glory*. "When he putts I want to turn my back, because he has developed a rather weird style. But it gets results. He is deadly on 4–6 foot putts."

Byron Nelson witnessed the same progress, returning to Glen Garden for a reunion match and finding Hogan to be the better man with the flat stick in his hand, at least from short distance. Furthermore, in 1955, when a *LIFE* magazine editor asked Nelson what he thought Hogan's secret was, Nelson answered, "driving and short putting."

These quotes from Dutra and Nelson are testament to Hogan's dedication to becoming a world-class putter, the best ever, and indicate that short putting was his forte early on. As for hitting and sinking medium-length putts and long putts with consistency, that journey would be a long and hard road. But this is something Hogan expected, since he was not just trying to learn a new putting stroke but inventing a whole new system. He would get there by doing things the old-fashioned way: through hard work and determination. Or, as Hogan was fond of saying, he "dug his game out of the dirt."

Starting out and, I'm sure, reminded by one of his mentors of the old Chinese proverb—"Every journey begins with a single step"—Hogan paid close attention to all his early instructors because each had something different on the putting game to share with the young up-and-coming golfer. But that does not mean Hogan accepted all. In fact, he filtered all the putting instruction he received meticulously, only incorporating into his system that which worked exceptionally well on the putting green first, and then, once it passed that test, out on the course.

In Jack Grout's case, Hogan conceded that Grout was a fundamentalist, but rather than repeating the same old hat instructional points, Grout approached the fundamentals from an entirely different angle. What impressed Hogan most, however, was the irony of Jack's teaching philosophy. In short, Grout's advice had more to do with the fundamentals of the prestroke routine than with stroke fundamentals.

Some of Jack Grout's more creative tips involved aiming at an intermediate dark or sparse spot on the designated line to the hole,

about halfway between the ball and the cup, just to take the pressure off needing to hole the putt. Staring at the interim spot allowed Hogan to relax, and feeling no pressure to hole the putt, he started sinking more medium-length putts, especially from the 10- to 15-foot range.

The most offbeat tip Hogan received from Grout related to green reading, which was shared with me by the late renowned editor, writer, and player Charles Price. If a green featured numerous slopes, and after reading the break from behind the ball and behind the hole looking back at the ball, and from both sides of the ball-hole line, you were still confused, Grout told his young pupil to stand as near as possible to the middle of the green without disturbing his fellow golfers, and to just imagine rain pelting down and flooding the putting surface. Then to look around and determine where the rainwater would run off and the speed at which it would leave the green. Now the player would be able to determine how the ball would break and get more than a rough idea about its speed.

HENRY PICARD was a leading tour player who made a couple of trips to visit Jack Grout at Glen Garden during the 1930s, in

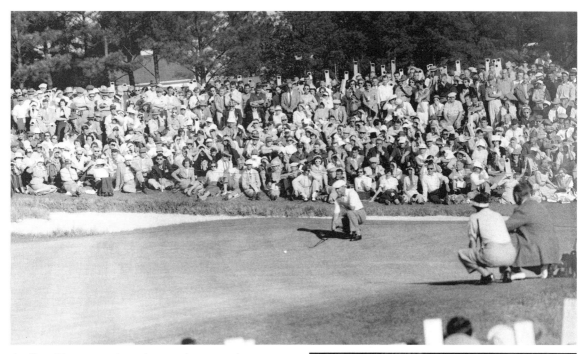

As Ben Hogan matured as a player and developed a solid putting stroke, he realized that one of the keys to evolving into an excellent putter, especially on super-fast surfaces, is to make certain you take the time during your prestroke routine (above) to pick an aiming spot on the green, halfway between the ball and the hole, and then hit the ball as firmly as you figured you would have to hit it to reach that spot. This insight was thanks to Jack Grout. Follow Hogan's instructions, even when putting out of light fringe-grass that borders a slick-green (right), and the ball will roll over your spot toward the hole and, seconds later, fall in.

order to exchange ideas on golf technique. It was at Glen Garden that Picard first met Hogan, and they began a relationship that stretched over many years. Hogan liked Picard's straightforward manner, the fact that he could prove what he preached about putting out on the course by sinking putts from various distances, and, most of all, his great experience and innovative mind.

Picard started off working for Alex Morrison, a teaching pro of the 1920s and 1930s who in 1923 established the first golf school in America, an indoor facility in New York City's Grand Central Terminal. Morrison, although a swing coach par excellence, taught Picard that certain fundamentals govern the putting setup and stroke, but that one can only take the basics so far. A fundamental, for example, governing a player's address, back-stroke, and down-stroke can change, depending on the putting situation. Furthermore, all will be lost unless a player personalizes his or her stroke by adding their own nuances. He or she must believe it all makes sense logically and they must be confident about swinging the putter correctly and sinking putts.

This type of thinking suited Picard, who

By the end of the 1930s, things started to click on the putting green in practice and out on the course during play.

was smart enough to realize early on, just by observing amateur and pro golfers putting, that different players employed different techniques when facing short, medium-length, and long putts. Yet, as sharp as Picard was, Hogan proved sharper. Hogan drew a different conclusion from these observations. Picard saw the various putting styles as simply personal, with each golfer having his or her way of doing things when hitting a particular type putt, and wrote it all off to choice and variations in human nature. Hogan, in contrast, concluded that while a foursome of golfers would all set up and stroke a putt of 25 feet that breaks right to left on a super-fast bent grass green differently, only one of the four players is setting up and stroking the putt in the best possible manner. This scenario served as the seed for Hogan's entire putting system, where he first dreamed up the idea of determining the best address, back-stroke, and down-stroke for each type of putt. This led to the discovery of four different strokes for handling different types of putting situations.

One of the reasons Hogan admired Picard so much and dedicated the book *Power Golf* to him was because of how

Picard phrased things having to do with putting instruction. Every word was special, and when Hogan put them all together, he discovered a message with a deeper meaning that encouraged him to start thinking outside the box and to look beyond sheer fundamentals in his search for the ideal putting system.

Hogan's favorite putting axioms, such as the ones that follow, all originate from something Picard said during a lesson and are designed to stimulate the golfer's brain and make the player think deeply about how he or she approaches the putting game:

• Once you have a putting stroke, a higher percentage of sinkable putts will start dropping for you regardless of whatever other individual idiosyncrasies you may have as a putter.

• Putting greens always slope away from the mountains on mountain courses because of weather and erosion. What you will have to guard against in reading greens on mountain courses, however, is little things which your knowledge of golf will tell you can't be true, although they appear to be so to the naked eye. You will learn what these things are only by experience.

• You should also develop your ability to tell the kinds of grasses on the green and their consistency through the feel of your feet on them as you walk around. Get so that you know the feel of the various grasses used on the greens and their relation to the speed of the ball, and that knowledge will be very helpful to you in learning how to putt.

• Remember in putting that the stroke can't do it all. You have to know how hard to hit the ball and where to aim it.

Ben Hogan went through almost the entire 1930s sacrificing playing time for practice time, but still competing often enough to know the true condition of his swing and total shot-making game, particularly putting.

In 1937, Grout left "The Garden" to work as assistant to Picard at the Hershey Country Club in Pennsylvania. At that point in his life Ben knew, more than ever, that it was time to take what putting fundamentals and nuances he had learned and expand his horizons outside of this club that had nurtured his golf game for so long.

By the end of the 1930s, things started to click on the putting green in practice and out on the course during play. Hogan's first professional win came in the 1938 Hershey Four-Ball with partner Vic Ghezzi. A win is a win, yes, but Hogan would rather have won a less notable 72-hole stroke-play tournament playing his own ball. Still, it was a start and, besides, meeting Ghezzi was a real turning point in Hogan's life. He was the one pro who encouraged Hogan to change putters, prior to Hogan's acquisition of the old faithful "brass doorknob" putter, telling Hogan the one he putted with was just too darn flat. Ghezzi, who sank the most putts in the tournament, played with a custom-fit putter he'd designed himself, and he sat Hogan down and told him all about the advantages of custom putters. Picard had mentioned this to Hogan earlier, of course, but because of Ghezzi's knowledge of clubs and Hogan's belief in that knowledge, he decided to make a switch. But surprisingly, this change would not happen overnight.

In 1939, Picard, fresh off wins at the 1938 Masters and 1939 PGA, teamed up with Jack Grout to win the Mid-South Four-Ball Championship at Pinehurst, putting into practice what they taught Ben Hogan and, ironically, what they learned from observing him. This boosted Hogan's confidence as well as convinced the young pro that he was making real progress toward developing a putting system that would help him and, he hoped, all golfers to shoot lower scores on the greens.

Hogan admitted, though, that he still had a long way to go. He would have to devise a prestroke routine in preparing to hit a putt and a basic setup position that combined elements of the fundamentals the Grout brothers and Picard had taught him but that also included personal nuances for addressing the ball, nuances that he found would change depending on the type of putt he faced and on what putting surface the ball was rolling on.

Consequently, Hogan would work on this part of his game for most of 1939, which explains why he did not win a single tournament that year. One of the ways he sought to improve his game was to pick the brains of great players in an attempt to glean applicable insight from their expertise. One of the players he approached was Bobby Locke, whose method of swinging the putter on a more rounded path and letting the toe of the putter head lead its heel at impact, so that hook-spin was imparted on the ball, worked really well. This kind of oblique strike of putter face to ball allowed Hogan—and will allow you—to hit long putts the proper distance without speeding up the natural tempo. This was the ideal solution to Hogan's problem of coming up short when hitting long putts on coarse, slow Bermuda grass greens or the ones at Carnoustie that he mastered using Locke's technique, thus helping him win The Open Championship of 1953.

In 1940, Picard gave up his job as playing professional for the Hershey Country Club. Hogan, whom Picard had highly recommended as a replacement, got the job. Hogan's new position afforded him more time to practice and compete in tournaments, but because he was still figuring things out with his swing and putting stroke (though, at times, he felt he was getting close to discovering the Holy Grail of golf technique), he just wasn't making enough progress—or money—and actually thought about packing it in, giving up playing professional golf for a living, and getting a real job.

Picard, having seen the improvements Hogan had made in his prestroke routine and setup position by virtue of the work he had done throughout 1939, encouraged Hogan to keep going. Picard cared so much about Hogan and his future that before he got on with his new life away from Hershey, he gave Hogan the assurance he needed, telling him that he would always be there for him if he needed help with his game and, more important, with financial backing.

According to Charles Price, the former editor of *GOLF Magazine* and *Golf Digest*, Picard knew Hogan would make it once he saw the work Hogan had done developing a prestroke routine for reading the breaks and grain in greens, judging speed, and visualizing the perfect putt; this was something Picard was fanatical about because he knew it was a common trait of golf champions. In fact, ever since Hogan had met Picard at Glen Garden, Picard recommended that Hogan observe the tour professionals who putted the most consistently well, to see for himself, so there would be absolutely no doubt in his mind that each great golf technician followed their own personalized prestroke putting routine.

The reason this process has such a positive influence on the actual putting stroke is that the more it is repeated over days, weeks, months, and years, the better equipped the player's mind is to recognize and accept precisely what movements of the body will be involved in the stroke, and what each will do and when, in a well-timed rhythmic sequence. Once the putting stroke is triggered, with a gentle pull on the grip with the right hand, which was Hogan's trigger, or by dipping the left shoulder so the right shoulder rises, the action will be put into motion and employed naturally, correctly, and automatically.

In short, as Picard explained to Hogan, it is only when you change an element of your prestroke routine, such as adding a couple more practice strokes than usual, or you do something out of sequence, such as employing practice strokes before you stare at the target to get a feel for how hard you must stroke the putt or how far the putter must be swung back, that the subconscious mind becomes confused. When that happens, the best putters will tell you, the stroke short-circuits. The more times this happens, the higher the likelihood of getting "the yips."

Thanks to the no-nonsense professional training Ben Hogan received at the Glen Garden Club, he developed a technically sound pure putting stroke that would serve as a template for the yip-proof four-stroke putting system detailed in subsequent chapters.

CHAPTER 4

HOGAN'S PROVEN PRESTROKE PLAN FOR PEAK PERFORMANCE

In preparing to putt, Ben Hogan put a whole lot of effort into "reading" a green's slopes and breaks, grain, speed of the putting surface, and narrowed his focus to Hole, Golf Ball, Putter.

The late Pat Ward-Thomas, a wonderfully gifted wordsmith who wrote a regular column on golf for the popular British magazine *Country Life*, once referred to the golf course as the "battlefield," where man is at war with all 18 holes. And if the golf course is a battlefield, then Hogan was a five-star general who, like Patton, was a student of war and warriors and believed, as Sun Tzu wrote in *The Art of War*, that "battles are won before they are fought."

Translated to golf, Hogan worked on a part of the game that, frankly, average amateur players take for granted and thus devote little time to when practicing or competing—the prestroke routine. This is a big mistake you do not want to make, as Hogan learned early on.

After some firm but friendly lecturing from mentor Henry Picard, Hogan started to look more seriously at what seemed a boring aspect of the game. After Picard proved how important the routine was to playing good golf more consistently, by winning the 1938 Masters and the 1939 PGA Championship, Ben began to map out a prestroke routine that he would depend on for the rest of his career.

Like anything one is required to build, whether it be a model airplane or a bird feeder, one must follow instructions: a step-by-step orderly plan. The prestroke routine encompasses the following critical elements:

• Reading break, grain, and speed of a green

• Picking a line to the hole that is determined by the contours or slopes or burrows in the green and also by how hard the ball is intended to be hit, plus one's sense of touch and experience putting on greens covered by different types of grass

• Visualizing that line

• Visualizing the ball you hit rolling along that line

• Concentrating with maximum focus on the ball and hole to visualize the ball falling into the cup

Always strategizing, Ben Hogan began analyzing the breaks in the putting surface when around 15 yards out from the green, as you can tell he is doing here from that familiar intense stare, all the while oblivious to the gallery.

All these steps constitute the prestroke routine to putting that Ben Hogan called "a matter of concentration, relaxation, and confidence."

The prestroke routine is the linchpin to the setup or starting position when putting or hitting any other shot. It is composed of the following elements: grip, stance, club face

Once he was on the putting surface and in the green-reading mode, one of Ben Hogan's trademarks when analyzing the break in a green was always to lay the putter down, virtually flat on the ground in front of him, as he does here, to get a strong sense of the line and its relationship to the target.

aim and body alignment, ball position, weight distribution, and position of the hands. The setup is the linchpin to the putting stroke because, essentially, the setup or address position predetermines the type of motion that is to be employed.

Whereas, respectfully, the novice believes that the prestroke routine is the same for all golfers, the experienced player knows that this is true only in general, not specific, terms. In short, the prestroke routine of one player can be better than the next, and quite different, too. And, without question, Ben Hogan's prestroke routine was second to none.

Why? Whereas almost all amateur golfers and the majority of professionals on tour start the prestroke routine when reaching the green, and then begin their read of what's before them in terms of break, for example, Ben Hogan started examining the green's contours when he was walking toward the green. The exact distance from the green he started depended on how good the light was and the degree of glare, or whether the sky was clear or overcast. Normally, Hogan started his read about 15 to 20 yards out from the putting surface, because he believed this strategy worked better than even an aerial view.

The average golfer looks at the break and the grain in a green from behind the ball looking toward the hole, as did Hogan.

However, Hogan also looked at the break from behind the hole looking back at the ball, from both sides of the line to the hole, and from around the hole too, looking for the direction of the grain and determining if the cup was set on a crowned area of the green or in a shallow dip.

Hogan was interested in these fine points of the prestroke routine, not just the basics, since he discovered early on that reading grain in a green and its contours is critical to the outcome of a putt, largely because of their relation to green speed, which directly impacts direction and where the ball ultimately ends up coming to rest.

Hogan, as with every other aspect of the game of golf, ended up becoming fanatical about the prestroke routine and was far superior as a strategist than all of his contemporaries save for perhaps Bobby Locke, whom Hogan acknowledged was the greatest putter he had ever seen when scoping out a green and preparing to putt. You don't need to become as fanatical, but it would sure help your putting game if you took the prestroke routine seriously. There is no doubt that a strong ability to read greens can save a golfer strokes on the course, improving his or her score.

Hogan wasn't the only one who recognized Locke's ability not only to sink putts but to read greens expertly. "Bobby Locke believed that most putts are missed not because they are mishit but because they are misread," wrote esteemed golf writer and editor Ken Bowden. "His first concern was pace, his second break, and [he] would not putt until he had a clear mental picture of the ball's speed and direction as it ran from him into the hole. Regarding pace, he had a definite rule of thumb for each texture of green. On a fast surface he tried to hit the ball as if the putt were six inches shorter than it really was; on a medium-paced green just to drop it over the front lip; and on slow greens to bounce it lightly off the back of the cup."

ONE OF the reasons Hogan's putting system came so close to perfection is because, right from the start of his journey, he tossed his ego out the window and was broad-minded enough to believe wholeheartedly that, while his own putting ideas were innovative, he did not have to solve all of the parts of the putting puzzle. Rather, Hogan studied the pre-stroke routines of the game's best putters, including Locke and Picard, and gleaned invaluable insights from them about grass grain—the direction in which grass grows or leans and how it affects the speed and direction of putts. A lot of the knowledge Ben gained about how to deal with grain emerged

from those observations and conversations. For example:

Step 1: Crouch down a yard or so behind the ball, with the sun at your back.

Step 2: Look closely at the grass between your ball and the hole.

A shiny look to the grass indicates that you are putting down-grain, with grass growing toward the hole, meaning the putt will roll more readily.

Hogan allowed for this grain factor and faster roll by contacting the ball close to the toe end of the putter, rather than on an area of the putter's face closer to the neck (where shaft meets putter head) to "deaden" the hit and, in turn, slow down the roll of the ball, as a countermeasure against a very fast-rolling ball that would otherwise be difficult to control.

In this same course situation, most amateur golfers make the mistake of hitting the ball too softly, employing a much shorter stroke, and making distance more difficult to control.

Dull grass means the grain is against you, thus the ball will roll more slowly than it would on a normal Bermuda grass putting green; it's kind of like putting on a shag carpet.

When Hogan was faced with hitting a putt into heavy grain, he simply contacted the ball atop its equator, with the sweet spot of the putter face. Such contact imparts

Here we see Ben Hogan doing his prestroke homework, looking for anything that could cause the putt he hits to be thrown off-line. Ben had to learn to accept one of the realities of golf, namely, that slight imperfections can be found even in the best greens, and that it's up to the player to look over his line to see and remove anything that can hinder the roll of the ball.

speed, will not always be to your liking. For that reason it's best to be prepared, as Ben Hogan learned in not the best of circumstances.

Following his back-to-back victories in the 1953 Masters and U.S. Open, Ben Hogan arrived in Scotland for The Open Championship at Carnoustie. Encountering greens that were much slower than those he was accustomed to, Hogan realized that he could either go home or go straight to the practice green. After unwisely mocking the course and offering to have lawn mowers sent in from Texas, Hogan chose to do the latter and won the championship.

Hogan was to realize, as did Bob Jones before him, that playing golf on a links course, on land once covered by water, is a whole new experience that can be exciting and enjoyable if you embrace the conditions. And although the greens have gotten faster over the years, they still are slower on the British Isles than we are accustomed to on this side of the Atlantic. Therefore, American golfers playing there can either lengthen their stroke, keep the same length stroke but hit their putts more firmly, use a heavier putter, contact the top half of the ball, or putt like Ben Hogan, who employed a slightly tweaked version of Bobby Locke's method, which we will examine in Chapter 6.

For the benefit of all you golfers who aren't able to get out on the course as often as

overspin on the ball and counteracts the slow speed of the green, via a faster roll of the ball.

Whether you prefer to putt on greens that roll at slow, medium, or fast speed, to become a complete golfer you will have no choice but to accept reality and know that sooner or later the conditions of the greens, in terms of an avid golfer does, let me make another important point about slow greens. In order for breaks in a slow green to play a major role in the way the ball curves and the speed at which the ball rolls, you'd have to be putting down a mountainside. The reason is that putting on slow greens is much easier than putting on fast greens.

Even a small slope in a speedy green will magnify, quite dramatically, the amount of break one has to negotiate and allow for. In contrast, on really slow greens you can practically aim right for the hole with little worry that the slope is going to have much effect on the rolling golf ball. For this reason, give me a putt of 20 feet on a slow sloped green any day over a 3-foot putt on a green as fast as one at Augusta National.

I've spoken to two South African golfers, Florida-based teaching guru Phil Ritson and the legendary Gary Player, about the putting prowess of Bobby Locke, their late fellow countryman and winner of four British Open championships. Phil is the best at spotting the smallest faults and the most subtle plus factors in a player's putting technique, while Gary invented and popularized the short, firm, hit-and-hold putting stroke.

Both men agree that Locke was the greatest long putter ever, but not just because he could read break, which again is not as critical on slow surfaces as it is on fast surfaces, but because he was the best at reading

speed—through his feet—which is something I believe Locke taught Hogan. However, this turned out to be only partially true. Although Locke was vigilant about checking out the surfaces he was putting on, and "listened" to the feedback he received through his feet, such as whether the greens were hard underfoot and thus fast-running, Picard was actually the first to teach Hogan to read a green's speed through his feet. In fact, Hogan acknowledged this in *Power Golf*, the book he dedicated to Picard.

"You should also develop your ability to tell the kinds of grass on the greens and their consistency through your feet as you walk around," Hogan wrote. "Get so you know the feel of various grasses used on the greens and the relation to the speed of the ball and that knowledge will be very helpful to your learning how to putt . . . remember, in putting, that the stroke can't do it all. You have to know how hard to hit the ball and where to hit it."

The most subtle points of the prestroke routine entail looking over the line to the hole, searching for any pebbles or heavier pieces of sand that may have been propelled onto the putting surface by a golfer playing in the group ahead of your foursome, such as when hitting a shot out of a bunker. There's also the chance that a tiny twig could have fallen off a tree and been blown onto the green and be sitting in your line to the hole; if not spotted and removed, it will likely

Whether hitting a left-to-right putt that you know from the contour in the green is going to curve quite dramatically (above, left) or a putt that you can tell from your read is going to turn severely from right to left (above, right), it's always better to follow the example set by Ben Hogan and play for more break on the high side of the curve, or "pro side" of the green, as opposed to the low side, below the crest of the curve, where the ball does not have a chance of dropping into the hole. Playing the ball on the high side offers you a bonus: If the ball ultimately fails to fall into the center of the cup, it still has a chance to drop into the "side door," on the side of the break, or even the "back door," at the back side of the cup, as its speed dies down to a near halt.

Here we see Ben Hogan watching every move Byron Nelson makes when putting, hoping to learn something new about the greens.

cause you to miss the putt. So be extremely vigilant, no matter how close you are to the hole and how good you are feeling. Like Ben Hogan, always keep your guard up.

Be sure to meticulously pick up anything on the line in which you intend to roll the ball to the hole, since it is against the rules of golf, as laid down by the United States Golf Association, to firmly brush the green's grass with the palm of your hand, and a penalty at a critical point in a match or tournament could prove costly.

The good news is that you are now permitted to brush the line gently with your fingers, hitting the top of each pebble and knocking them out of your line, although better etiquette would entail you picking up each small pebble, one by one, and tossing them into the nearby woods or water hazard, as a courtesy to the golfers playing behind your group.

You'll also be penalized if you stamp down a spike mark in your line, even though it seems unfair that you should lose a match or a tournament or fail to break your own personal scoring record because the ball you putted hit a spike mark left by a player up ahead who dragged his or her feet across the green. Fortunately, now that many players choose or are forced to wear soft spikes because of local rules, spike marks are rarer, at least as we knew them.

Should a spike mark hinder your line to the hole on short putts, do what Hogan used to do in this situation: Stroke the ball more firmly to mitigate the effect the spike mark will have on the rolling ball.

On long breaking putts on fast greens, Hogan was savvy enough to allow for an additional amount of break and hit the ball more easily, so that it rolled around or wide of the spike mark scar and, ideally, caught the "side door" of the hole. Follow Hogan's example as well as that of Jack Nicklaus, who I've seen do the same in this situation.

In order to get Hogan's brain working fully, with maximum concentration and spot-on focus, Picard played off Hogan's competitive spirit prior to triggering his stroke and turned the subject of discussion into a challenge. In addition to stressing to Hogan that proper prestroke planning promotes peak performance putting, Picard brought the element of competition into the "lesson," even going so far as to say the course superintendent sometimes purposely cut the cup on a crowned area of the green that's the

Veteran players like Sam Snead and Claude Harmon knew that when they saw Ben Hogan in a casual pose like this, it was a sign that he'd figured out the line to the hole and visualized the ball dropping into the hole, and as soon as it came his turn to putt, you could pretty much guarantee that Hogan was going to step up and make that positive image of sinking a birdie putt come true.

slowest part of the putting surface to test the golfer's strategic and physical skills. This challenged Hogan to outsmart the "super" and win the chess game. Hogan did this by going through a prestroke checklist or routine that included making a promise to himself not to set up to the ball, let alone start the putting stroke, before being fully satisfied

FIVE LESSONS:
THE MODERN FUNDAMENTALS OF PUTTING

LESSON 1:
A TEACHER-STUDENT/ STUDENT-TEACHER RELATIONSHIP LIKE NO OTHER

Following years of research and grueling trial-and-error practice, Ben Hogan finally arrived at a four-stroke system of putting that only one other golfer in the world was using to sink putts and win tournaments—lots of tournaments. It just so happened that this player had also taken putting lessons from pros Jack Grout and Jack Burke Jr., had played with Hogan whenever he could, and admitted in his autobiography, *The Greatest Game of All*, that every time they ventured out on the golf course together he learned something new from Hogan. That student's name was Jack Nicklaus, whose progress Hogan had tracked faithfully. Hogan had noticed

Ben Hogan during a practice round at Augusta National, watching closely as the star "student"—the one and only Jack Nicklaus—makes a putt. Only this time, in 1966, Hogan learned something from Nicklaus about golf's "ground game" that enabled him to do something spectacular the following year at the Masters Tournament.

sometime after their first round of golf together, in the 1960 U.S. Open, that Nicklaus had started looking more and more like him when putting.

When you appreciate that Hogan had already had some guidance from the head professional at Glen Garden, Dick Grout, and his brother, Jack (who had started teaching Nicklaus when Nicklaus was 11 years old), the picture starts taking shape. Furthermore, when you consider that Jack Grout knew Hogan's putting techniques inside and out well before he started teaching Nicklaus, you start seeing the picture really clearly.

As time went on, Jack added his own nuances to the Hogan method—one in the setup and one in the prestroke routine—that Hogan was happy to see. Specifically, Jack held the putter just above the surface of the green, believing this made for a smoother takeaway; employed a "forward press" action, in the form of a firming of the grip, to trigger the transition between the address and back-stroke (which Hogan liked so much he copied); and contacted the ball higher up the putter's face, thereby producing a smoothly rolling ball, with no "skidding" or bouncing occurring after impact.

Lifting the putter off the ground is a good idea, in the sense that if you are getting ready to putt and the ball moves, you cannot be penalized (technically, according to the

This type of club face-to-ball contact, shown from two angles (above), is a feature of Jack Nicklaus's putting game that proved to be a real plus factor. Ben Hogan preferred doing the same thing, but mainly when hitting short and medium-length putts on slow greens (below).

Rules of Golf, one has not officially addressed the ball until the club is grounded). On the other hand, Hogan believed Jack's "up" position of the putter created tension in the arms. That can lead to the problem of deceleration in the putting stroke. Again, what's good about that position is the roll it gives to the ball.

Ben Hogan had followed Nicklaus's career, always answering Jack's questions when they played together but never saying anything about the similarity in the strokes, not even after Hogan noticed, in 1962, that Nicklaus changed his right-hand grip from weak to more in the palm, or "strong," but still kept his thumb straight down the shaft as Hogan did.

When Jack shot "lights out" and holed several birdie putts en route to his incredible 1986 Masters win, making minor changes for short, medium-length, and long putts, Hogan knew he had invented the perfect putting system. All the same, I have studied Nicklaus, and there are other putting actions that Hogan employed that Jack did not, and which golfers can learn from.

No matter how good a putter Ben Hogan was during his heyday, and no matter how good a putter Jack Nicklaus turned out to be, it's interesting to study Hogan's stroke, then Nicklaus's, for similarities and differences.

LESSON 2:
TICK-TOCK, TICK-TOCK

Once out of the blue, in 1950 Hogan came home from practicing one day and wondered why his distance control on long putts was off. He pondered how to remedy this problem of hitting putts short of the hole. After meditating on it for about a week and trying out some new things, he concluded that the problem he was having pacing long putts, particularly those in the 25- to 45-foot range, was being caused by a problem in his grip, namely, squeezing the club too tightly.

According to Herbert Warren Wind, Hogan also had the sense that his putting stroke felt robot-like; he just did not feel right and, as a result, was still failing to hit long putts solidly enough. After Hogan practiced some more, his wife, Valerie, of all people, noticed that his back-stroke was faster than his down-stroke. His tempo was off.

Hogan found an unusual solution to this problem. His friend, the pianist of *Casablanca* fame, Hoagy Carmichael, suggested that Hogan do two things to improve his distance control on long putts:

1. Carmichael suggested that Hogan work out on the putting green with a metronome to even out the pace between his

The reason Ben Hogan became so good at hitting long putts (above, left) was due to the "secret weapons" pianist Hoagy Carmichael, seen here walking with Hogan (above, right), recommended he try: a metronome and ginger beer.

back-stroke and down-stroke, and keep working with it until he felt that the speed going back and the speed coming through were the same. Hogan bought into this, because he never changed speed on long putts, especially when putting on bent grass greens. He employed a longer stroke, and he also had some success hitting the top half of the ball. And on Bermuda grass greens that were especially slow, Hogan eventually started using the Bobby Locke technique of imparting a degree of hook-spin on the ball.

According to Herbert Warren Wind, Hogan used the metronome to even out his tempo for all putts, because he never changed his tempo, only the type of stroke he employed and the way he came into impact. That's how he controlled speed, which is savvy strategy.

2. Carmichael suggested that Hogan start drinking ginger beer, something Hogan had never heard of, because it removes the puffiness from one's fingers so that one's sense of touch and feel for the swinging putter and distance are enhanced. Hogan later made a reference to ginger ale (which was much easier to find than ginger beer) in *Five Lessons*, writing that it "seems to prevent the hands from feeling too fat and puffy." You can now find ginger beer—which tastes like very strong ginger ale—in good grocery and health food stores.

Putting at a piece of luggage in a hotel room or rented home (above), hitting putts with a sprinkler running full blast near the practice putting green (opposite, top), and putting when the light is going down (opposite, bottom), were examples of the kind of outside-the-box practice that made Ben Hogan a putting champion. (Note how Ben addresses the ball close to the putters neck, as opposed to its center. The "sweet spot" is located below that point where the shaft meets the putter-head.

LESSON 3:
OUTSIDE-THE-BOX PRACTICE

One of the first photographs I came across when I began researching this book showed Byron Nelson and Ben Hogan practicing in the cold weather at the Glen Garden Club. Hogan likely convinced Byron that, since you never know what the course conditions are going to be like, it's best to be prepared for the worst.

As it turned out, when Hogan played in The Open Championship in 1953 at Carnoustie, in Scotland, it was freezing, with conditions so shockingly bad that most players were thrown off their games. But because Hogan had rehearsed this very situation in practice, he was able to endure the cold weather and went on to win the British Open in fine style, including shooting a competitive course record 68 on the last day.

Well, I found out Hogan did some even weirder things to prepare for bad conditions, things that also helped him hone the three areas that matter so much to good putting: concentration, confidence, and relaxation.

Drills Hogan would work on included purposely trying to ease the ball to the "baseline" of a small piece of luggage in his hotel room, in order to hone his "die putt" stroke. This drill was designed to feed the ball to the hole such that it just fell over the edge of the cup, then dropped slowly into it, as if everything was in slow motion. Hogan also hit putts with the sprinklers running nearby to get used to distractions and learn to block them out by concentrating really hard. He would practice in the early evening when the sun was starting to go down, so that he was prepared in case the round ran late due to earlier delays caused by lightning or heavy rain slowing play, or in case he was part of a sudden-death playoff.

Hogan, who was known to arrive at a major championship venue a week in advance, would also practice shots he'd rarely have to execute in tournament play. For example, at Augusta he would find a lie near the green, in the first cut of fringe, where he could practice putting from and then compare it to chips played with other clubs to see if the putter was better, just in case he got in that situation during the tournament.

When Hogan was working on something new for his putting system, he'd go out and practice alone, hitting putts where he figured the holes would be "cut" on each of the 4 days of a major championship. Going out to the course alone, a few days before the competition started, allowed him to hit several putts from different spots on a green without having to worry about being courteous to fellow players. That wasn't Hogan's style. He preferred to practice until he pretty much attained perfection. Besides, during a major championship in particular, Hogan only thought about himself, the course, and winning.

LESSON 4:
WHAT YOU SEE IS WHAT YOU GET

Ben Hogan's life and career was a roller coaster ride, I suppose starting with the deep wound he suffered in 1921, when he witnessed the suicide of his father, Chester. Hogan found a new life as a caddie at the Glen Garden Club in Fort Worth, Texas, and with guidance from head professional Dick Grout and, later, Dick's brother, Jack, along with Henry Picard, Hogan was in the ideal training facility—a boot camp of sorts.

Encouraged by his progress, Hogan turned pro in 1931, at age 19, and looking for further guidance he returned occasionally to play Glen Garden and visit his mentors. By 1937, Hogan was flat broke. Marvin Leonard, founder of Colonial Golf Club, also in Fort Worth, bailed out the Hogans, while further moral support and the promise of additional financial help came from Henry Picard.

In 1946 and 1948, Hogan proved to himself that he had what it takes to win a major championship and earn a living on tour, taking home the PGA Championship both years.

In winning the 1950 United States Open trophy in one of the greatest comeback stories ever, Ben Hogan knew he'd made another putting breakthrough—and Sam Snead was one pro who knew we'd be hearing more from him.

Jimmy Demaret's off-beat advice to get Ben Hogan out of feeling stuck in the putting address—to visualize swinging a driver to the at-the-top position (above, left), then swinging through the ball into the follow-through (above, right)—cured Hogan's problem right away.

Hogan was proud of both of his PGA wins, but there was something else he was excited about. Hogan told Sam Snead that, in beating Mike Turnesa by the huge margin of 7 & 6 at the 1948 PGA, he realized some things about putting that really clicked—namely, that the short stroke and the long stroke are not the same, and that if you try to hit a long putt with the same stroke you use on a short putt, you will never be a consistently good putter.

Then, just as the world was beginning to become his oyster, Ben Hogan and his wife were involved in a head-on collision with a Greyhound bus. The story of Hogan's trials and tribulations and comeback that started with a win in the 1950 U.S. Open has been well documented in several books and in the wonderful film *Follow the Sun*, starring Glenn Ford. That's what you know. But here's something I doubt you do, unless Sam Snead told you what he told me that he said to Hogan after his comeback win at the 1950 U.S. Open: "Ben, I gotta give it to you. I guess you sure did find that something special at the 1948 PGA."

Well, with golf being the fickle sport it is, Hogan still had some more work to do. The years 1951 and 1952 were dry ones for him. But, as he had done before, he shut everybody up the following year, with his golf clubs doing the talking.

This may not have happened had he not gotten a new tip and a pep talk from a fellow competitor, three-time Masters champion Jimmy Demaret. Demaret and Hogan were known to kid each other, but this time the matter was serious, and Demaret thought it had something to do with Hogan's accident. Hogan was feeling uncomfortable over putts, particularly putts from 10 feet and in, and as a result, was making an overly short back-stroke and not hitting through the putt.

"Ben," Demaret said, "the next time you stand over these type putts, thinking you are going to freeze, I want you to do two things after you have set up to the ball and picked out a line. First, visualize yourself employing a full backswing and an accelerating follow-through. Next, start your stroke and you'll never have the problem you had again, because this type imagery will make you swing the putter back freely and through freely and not worry about anything else."

The advice worked, and Ben Hogan never forgot it.

In 1953, Hogan captured the only three major championships he entered: the Masters, the United States Open, and The Open Championship (British Open). Quite a trifecta.

LESSON 5: HELP FROM ANOTHER GOLFER NAMED JACK

One does not need to read the works of Carl Jung to conclude that Hogan's recurring dream, in which he scored aces on 17 consecutive holes before lipping out on 18, and waking up angry about failing to play the perfect round, indicates that, to Hogan, learning golf meant mastering the game through a lifetime process.

As it pertained to his putting game, Ben Hogan sought to accomplish this ambitious goal through tireless experimentation on the putting green, in his living room, and in hotel rooms and hotel hallways when on the road; by looking at old photographs in books and magazines showing golfers putting; plus talking to the best putters in the game, such as Bobby Locke, Claude Harmon, two of the most talented teachers he grew up with at Glen Garden, Dick and Jack Grout, as well as Henry Picard, Jimmy Demaret, and a man who liked to remain low-key and still does, yet is one of the finest players and teachers in the world, the 1956 Masters and PGA champion: Jack Burke Jr.

While Burke will never take credit for helping Jack Nicklaus or Ben Hogan, the fact is he helped them both. Nicklaus speaks about how Burke helped him by suggesting

When Jack Burke Jr. putted, Ben Hogan was all eyes, looking to see how Burke employed a practice stroke and stroked his putts by employing a natural-feeling, easy-to-repeat right-sided putting action that Burke helped Hogan refine, as in the accompanying photographs.

he alter his right-hand grip, such that he could better push the club through the impact area. When you turn the right hand under the club in a stronger position, yet still keep your right thumb down the shaft, it is far easier to employ the push action that Nicklaus putted so well with in tournaments and major championships.

The irony is that Hogan learned the palm-grip position and stroke action before Nicklaus; in fact, Hogan learned it in 1960, 2 years before Jack was given a putting lesson from Burke. I have gathered photos that show Hogan and Burke working together on putting technique on the practice green of Augusta National during the 1960 Masters. As you can see from the accompanying photographs, Burke demonstrates the proper setup position and stroke while Hogan watches, then Hogan sets up and

When Ben Hogan tries to emulate "Jackie," Burke watches Hogan carefully, making sure his setup and stroke techniques are up to the strict standard Hogan demands of himself, as in the accompanying photographs.

strokes short putts, employing the all-important right palm–right forearm push action through impact, while Burke watches.

Hogan's weak left hand and strong right, his head position with eyes over the target line behind the ball, 80% of his lower-body weight on the left foot in what he calls the anchor position, the back of his left hand slightly ahead of the ball, and elbows bent in close to his body are all setup positions that must be checked.

On the back-stroke, the priority in checking technique is to be sure that Hogan keeps his body still and works off a hinge action of the right wrist while making sure that the club swings back along the target line, never in an

exaggerated shut position (pointing down at the target line on a sharp, oblique angle), but square to the hole, and never dramatically along a path inside the target line.

On the down-stroke, the priorities in checking technique relate specifically to making sure that the right wrist straightens in time with the push triggers of the right forearm and palm, and that the club returns along the same line it swung back along. It should be returned in a streamlined manner, too. You should never hit down on the ball. I have seen only one pro make this work, through various compensatory moves and much manipulation of the putter: Isao Aoki. But make no mistake: There are far easier

ways to putt well, as Ben Hogan proved over and over again thanks to some special things he learned early on from studying pictures of Australian amateur great Walter Travis and then later in his career from Jack Burke Jr.— and Jack Nicklaus!

While the setup of Travis, the weak left-hand and strong right-hand grip, and the right-wrist-hinge back-stroke trigger he employed all helped Hogan greatly, the refinements of the address and putting stroke came from Burke. The latter was such a help to Hogan at the Masters in 1960 that a few months later Hogan almost won the United States Open for a record fifth time.

Hogan's tournament days were virtually

over. Yet there he was in April, working with Burke, trying to perfect a stroke in his system. And, yes, he could have won that Open. But the fact is, Hogan really wanted to develop a new system that could help all golfers. And he was working on this quietly, behind the scenes, just like what my friend Greg Hood told me Hogan used to do without anyone else knowing about it, without wanting any credit: While he was owner of the Ben Hogan Golf Company, he used to pack his car with sets of brand-new clubs and drop them off in poor neighborhoods.

No wonder Jack Burke Jr. and Ben Hogan were such good friends. Both were givers, not takers. The world needs more people like that.

that he had considered all of the variables that influence the direction and speed of the ball on the green, such as the break and grain of the grass.

While all this sounds like a lot of trouble to go through, Tiger Woods's longtime amateur coach, John Anselmo, captured the importance of the prestroke routine when, in his book *A-Game Golf,* he wrote, "A putt can be missed or made long before the ball is struck with the putter face."

Your lesson: If you fail to put in the effort of going through your prestroke preparation, in a step-by-step, organized fashion, much like a pilot does before takeoff, you will inevitably fail to read the green properly, step into your address unprepared and incorrectly, and then likely miss the putt.

IN POINTING out what a practiced preparer Ben Hogan had become by the early 1950s, Desmond Tolhurst, author and former instruction editor of *GOLF Magazine,* told me that before a major championship Hogan would have breakfast and then play a round of golf, hitting a few balls off every tee, to determine where the best landing area was to establish the best angle into the hole for various pin placements.

Late in the afternoon, during practice rounds before a major, when the sun was lower off the horizon, Hogan would walk the course and stop almost 15 yards from each green, in the center of the short grass, and from this vantage point make notes in a little memo pad he would carry in his back pocket during the championship. He noted things such as which way the green sloped and whether there was anything out of the ordinary, like a small bowl area or hump in the green that he'd rather avoid by hitting his approach shot either short or long.

Now that's preparation—sort of a pre-prestroke routine!

ONE INTERESTING observation Sam Snead made when analyzing Hogan's putting game was that if he did miss, he always missed well up on the high side of the hole rather than on the low side, or what's typically referred to by veteran golfers as the "amateur side."

Knowing that putts break more dramatically on fast greens than on slow greens, where the longer blades slow the ball's sideways and forward movement, will help you make adjustments in your aim. In short, to counter this, simply aim more to one side. If unsure of the break, you should also allow for more break, as Ben Hogan did, since the ball could still fall into the "side door."

Here we see Ben Hogan in "The Zone," staring up at the hole, visualizing the line one last time.

In closely observing Ben Hogan's putting game, Byron Nelson once told me that Hogan was the "Desert Fox" of golf, always looking for an advantage, a way to take control of a match or tournament. Nelson noticed that Hogan seemed to scrutinize every other pro he was playing with who showed prowess with the putter, watching every stroke and the tempo of the stroke, to the point of never stopping staring until the ball stopped rolling.

"I and every other guy out on tour almost always looked away, scared to be misled by another player's stroke and speed of the stroke and ball," Nelson said. "But, when I asked Ben why he was so keen on watching, he just told me that the plus factors outweigh the minus factors, then walked away."

What I gathered from this story is that Hogan was telling Nelson, in his own short and stern manner, to do his own homework, his way, and that if you watch the other players in your group really closely, you probably can learn something about the speed and breaks in the green that can help you—if not on that day, then during a subsequent round.

MIND CONTROL

While Ben Hogan never admitted that he was ever hypnotized to alleviate the memory of his horrific car crash, or to overcome the severe back pain, nightmares, night sweats, and stress this near-fatal accident ushered in, Tom Scott, the late golf editor and author who I worked with at *Golf Illustrated* in London, had always been convinced that Hogan surely utilized some form of mind control when competing in major championships. He based this theory on hearing from a caddie who witnessed Hogan, after a session hitting balls on the practice tee of Augusta, working with a metronome.

The caddie told Scott that when Hogan completed his private session, readying himself for a tournament round, he seemed to be a different person, off in his own little world, where he remained for the entire 18 holes. Tick-tock, tick-tock, tick-tock: I suppose this musical training gadget could literally click one into a hypnotic state. As I learned when writing the book *Think Like Tiger*, which explored hypnosis and zen meditation as it pertained to Tiger Woods, hypnotism always requires some kind of trigger.

While on the subject of Tiger, the square-to-square putting stroke that he employed during his winning years, when he captured 14 major championships, was practically identical to Ben Hogan's short/medium-length stroke, except that Tiger shut the face down in the back-stroke to keep it square, giving us the hint that there was some manipulation present. The face of Hogan's putter remained square all the way, from the start to the finish of the stroke, because he

Hogan looks down at the ball one last time before he triggers the putting stroke with a gentle pull on the putter's handle with his right hand.

locked his arms into his body and moved the club back with a gentle pull with the right hand and a hinging of the right wrist, then pushed it through with his right palm and right forearm, while straightening the right wrist, at a speed that very gradually became more up-tempo as the length of the putt increased. All the same, as nonmanipulative as this stroke was, and no matter how much better I believe it was than Tiger's, Hogan

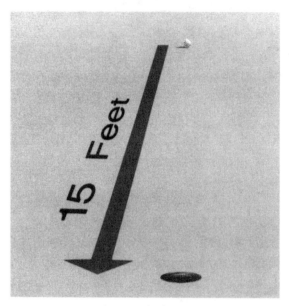

When you look at your ball sitting on the green and then the hole, and you have to hit the ball into the hole (above) to win the match or tournament, and you feel your heart rate go up and your hands start to sweat, imagine a bigger size hole (below).

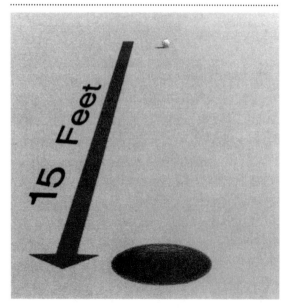

could never have holed out so many times under the pressure of major championship golf had he not depended on mind-control.

Personally, because Hogan was always doing something different, using a metronome to click himself into "The Zone" would not surprise me one bit, especially since I have been told by various golf insiders (such as one of golf's longest hitters ever, Mike Austin, who admitted to being hypnotized) about how, once play started in a major championship, Hogan had a faraway look in his eyes, an enlightened gleam, which, at least partially, does relate to Hogan's deep belief in the Lord.

It sure is no secret that when standing on the tee preparing to drive, readying himself to hit an approach shot, or while staring at the hole one last time before triggering the putting stroke, a cigarette dangling from his lips, Hogan seemed to be in a trance, a cocoon of concentration. What's even more interesting, and lends this metronome story credibility, is that while conducting research for this book, I found out from Herbert Warren Wind that Hogan did use a metronome to help him stroke putts more smoothly. So perhaps the metronome had a dual purpose.

Hogan obviously had his game under control, having won so many golf tournaments, and some golfers will say that's all that matters. That is for you, and you alone, to decide.

I will say this much: The metronome issue aside, it was around 1950 that those who knew Hogan said he had a different look in his eyes—Sam Snead, for one.

This makes sense, not only because Hogan spoke of the Lord, but because during the major championships following the recovery period after his crash, Hogan's whole facial expression and body language changed dramatically. According to Snead, "It seemed sacks of potatoes had been taken off Hogan's back, but I always believed this to be just his being lucky and happy to be alive."

Considering Ben Hogan's relaxed state of mind, whether we call it "The Zone" or whether it was triggered by a hypnotic code or the Lord's Prayer, the fact is that a relaxed body and an anxiety-free mind are essential to good golf. In talking to sports psychologist Glen Albaugh, as well as golf pro Scott McCarron, who was working with Glen at the time I interviewed him, here's how their thinking applies to Ben Hogan.

One super-positive aspect of Ben Hogan's game was how he approached each putt as a new hole with a par of one or two, depending on its length and difficulty. Setting up to the putt with 100% confidence, knowing he had practiced the address and stroke over and over, emboldened him with the courage to let go. His confidence had nothing to do with his performance, whether favorable or unfavorable, on the previous hole.

When I spoke with Albaugh about this zone some athletes are able to enter, he attributed it less to an externally triggered hypnotic state than to a super-high resulting from putting oneself into a state of supreme confidence. Applying what Albaugh taught me, I believe that Hogan must have discovered what Albaugh believes—that feeling confident over a putt should not depend on any previous putt. Instead, as Albaugh explained, confidence is a state of mind you can learn to put yourself in through what Tim Gallwey, author of *The Inner Game of Golf*, calls "self-talk."

Albaugh is very big on positive imagery and absolute trust, with the latter being something I believe is essential to good mental health on the golf course and good putting. This high state of confidence is the first step to entering "The Zone."

Having said this, with Ben Hogan enduring so much pain as a child, then the car crash, I don't see how he could have just instilled this sense of confidence into his whole being. To me, he needed the help of "the Lord"—his words, not mine—and/or some form of hypnosis. Later, once he starting building his putting system and seeing it work, I have no doubt that he did what Albaugh suggests: generate his own state of confidence. Or maybe his faith in the Lord allowed him to become confident before he had seen positive results from his system. This, unfortunately, we shall never know. But that does not stop us from realizing the importance of golf's mental side and how it helped Hogan sink more putts, whatever its origin.

Trust in one's ability to putt well is a definite key to entering "The Zone." The secret to trusting your putting setup and putting stroke to operate for you on the golf course, especially in pressure situations, is to let go, to give up conscious control of the putting stroke. This is something else Albaugh is big on, as is Yvon Legault, an exceptionally talented putting coach based in Canada. Legault has studied Hogan and believes learned techniques are used by the reactive subconscious. Trust allows your body to relax. A relaxed golfer is more likely to drop his defenses and let his subconscious control the coordinated movement of the body and club. And, if you do feel extra pressure on the green when standing over a putt and looking at the hole and then back down at the ball, look back at the hole again, one last time, before triggering the putting stroke, then do what Ben Hogan did in pressure situations on the green: Imagine that the hole is two to three times bigger.

AS FOR getting the basics of Hogan's four-stroke technique down pat, you must first understand each component intellectually, then drum each of the strokes you have learned something about already into your muscle memory, so you can employ each movement without thinking about the specific elements involved in the stroke. I bring this up here because of its mental game applications and so you can see its value and why it will pay off for you as it did for Ben Hogan.

Just as an actor is able to do a better job immersing himself in a character when he has his lines down cold, you, like Hogan in his heyday, will be better able to employ all of the necessary physical actions involved in putting if you have previously practiced the total stroke action enough times for it to be repeated easily and naturally on the golf course without having to connect the dots mentally. This is what is meant by letting go: trusting your putting stroke to be directed by the subconscious, and operating on automatic pilot.

YOUR POSTSTROKE PLAN FOR PEAK PERFORMANCE

Part of putting the Hogan way entails forgetting about making a bad stroke and missing the hole (below), leaving a putt short (top, right), or missing a putt to one side due to a misread or mishit (below, right), and doing what he learned to do (and what Jack Nicklaus also had a tremendous capacity for) when things failed to go his way on the green.

Walk off the green and imagine a door closing (right) and, immediately, begin to focus on the next shot, which is the only shot you can control.

CHAPTER 5
NATURAL SELECTION

It is no coincidence that Ben Hogan won 63 tournaments, including 9 major championships, using a custom-fit putter. All things being equal, the golfer who putts with a custom putter tailored to one's comfortably correct setup and natural stroke tendencies will perform best on the greens of any golf course.

By the time Ben Hogan turned professional in 1931, golf course maintenance had become a big business in America. Wealthy golfers, tired of the slow speeds of longish-cut, uneven greens, had pushed in the previous decade for their club executives to purchase and utilize with regularity the motorized lawn mowers that had recently become available to the general public, changing the course of golf forever.

For a variety of reasons, the speed of greens varied from course to course in those days, sometimes subtly, sometimes dramatically. What left young Hogan scratching his head were the paradoxes and exceptions relative to these speeds. Just because a golf course featured Bermuda grass greens did not mean the golf ball would roll slowly across its surface. By the same token, a golf course featuring bent grass greens did not guarantee that the ball would roll briskly across its putting surface. Let's look at why that was true.

Members of a club in Florida, for example, could demand that the course superintendent shave the normally slow, coarse Bermuda grass greens, common in the South, real low so the ball rolled quite quickly over these newly manicured, smooth surfaces. Likewise, the smooth bent grass greens common to the northeastern region of America, which Ben had found to be more to his liking, sometimes were slow-rolling. This was particularly true of a less-affluent private club lacking the maintenance budget to keep the greens on its course mowed low. It was also quite common for owners of a public course to instruct the maintenance crew to refrain from cutting the greens down too low, owing to heavy play and wanting to protect the putting surfaces from becoming threadbare and eventually ruined by excessive wear and tear.

These changing conditions signaled to Hogan that while lighter steel-shaft putters, in a wide array of new styles and ideal for putting on fast greens, were increasing in popularity, there was still a place in the game for heavy putters, albeit ones now featuring steel shafts.

In 1934 and 1935, Lawson Little, a California amateur golfer, stunned the golf world by winning the United States and British amateur titles 2 years running. Little's long hitting, particularly off the tee, pumped up golfers—which was nothing new. What was new was that Little's great putting, performed with a steel-shaft putter, brought the precision mind-set to golf and stirred new interest in it from the public and private sector, with a multitude of sports-minded persons realizing golf was more than just a macho game.

Little's great performance proved inspirational to Ben Hogan, and soon after he began devoting more time to putting practice, mostly of the experimental kind, and also started to concentrate more on learning about the chief elements of a putter that represented the specs of a custom fit.

Following the war, during which his golf career was interrupted by a 2-year stint in the Army Air Force, Hogan sank birdie putts from practically everywhere on the greens (particularly at the 1948 PGA Championship), giving him the incentive to press on and work harder to develop and perfect a new system of putting.

As excited as Hogan was about winning a second PGA title, he was even more excited about feeling something positive "click" in his putting stroke, particularly during the final match when his birdie barrage closed out opponent Mike Turnesa, a fine golfer, by the huge margin of 7 & 6. Hogan experienced the sensation of the body working in harmony with the movement of the putter, in such a coordinated and synchronized manner, that the entire motion felt effortless. He was experienced enough to know that whenever a golfer experiences this sensation, it's a sure sign that his stroke is working at maximum efficiency.

But just as Hogan was poised to follow up on these mental and physical leads and take his game to the next level, he was nearly killed when, in February 1949, his car was struck head-on by a Greyhound bus.

Recuperating at home after several months in the hospital, Hogan meditated on all aspects of his golf game and his life. It was then that he first came to the conclusion that he had to find ways to handle both super-sloped and super-slow greens if he was ever going to discover a revolutionary putting system that would allow him to win major championships other than the PGA and U.S. Open—namely, the Masters (super-sloped) and the British Open (super-slow).

Recalling a conversation with mentor Henry Picard, in which Picard had casually commented on how personal putting is and how strokes differ dramatically in terms of style, a buzzer went off in Hogan's head. It was a wakeup call that told Hogan he must develop a system of multiple putting strokes that would allow him to go about the business of sinking putts on a variety of surfaces at varying distances and varying speeds. The challenge was made more demanding at this juncture of Hogan's golf career because he was confused about what one putter to carry in his golf bag: the upright blade putter he used to win over 20 tournaments (Putter #1, for easy identification in these pages) or the flat-lie blade putter that helped contribute to that click feeling he experienced when putting so well en route to winning the 1948 PGA Championship (Putter #2).

Putter #1 was an upright, customized putter that was fairly light and measured 38 inches, 2 inches longer than standard. It featured a simple-looking head design and boasted a thin steel shaft in a medium-flex, a long, thin leather grip, 2 degrees of loft built into the putter's face, and a lie angle of 3 degrees more upright than standard. It weighed in at D-2 on the swing-weight

> As excited as Hogan was about winning a second PGA title, he was even more excited about feeling something positive "click" in his putting stroke.

scale. This is the putter Hogan can be seen using in the putting photos that appear in *Power Golf.*

By this time, Hogan had already developed, yet not perfected, the square-to-square stroke that could be called a hinge-and-release action, where the movement of the putter is controlled by the hinging action of the right wrist on the back-stroke and then the releasing or straightening action of the right wrist on the down-stroke. The more Hogan employed this straight back-straight through square-stroke, in practice and in play, the more he realized that this type of putting stroke, ideal for hitting short and medium-length putts, deserved to be the first technique included in the putting system he was developing.

Over time, however, after much experimentation with both putters, Hogan realized that, due to the different putting situations he was sure to encounter on the greens during a typical round of competitive golf, the one putter he needed to carry in his bag was one he felt was the most versatile and that was not so upright that it would prevent him from employing an inside-stroke on long putts, yet not so flat that it would prevent him from employing a square-stroke on short and medium-length putts. That designation went to Putter #2, the putter Hogan is gripping on the cover of this book.

Having said this, this is one of the times in Hogan's life when he actually thought seriously of carrying two putters: Putter #1, the upright model, ideal for short and medium-length putts, and Putter #2, the flat-lie model, ideal for long putts.

Hogan chose Putter #2 as his official putter because its slightly flatter lie angle allowed him to employ the second type of main stroke that would become part of his putting system, an inside-down the line action, ideal for long putts while also allowing him to employ his square-to-square stroke for short and medium-length putts. Putter #2, for all you equipment buffs, is a hand crafted custom-fit putter, constructed of a solid brass putter head, in a design that's a cross between two classic putters, the Spalding "Cash-In" and the Titleist "Bull's Eye." Hogan used this putter to win all his major championships contested under stroke-play format. It registered D-5 on the swing-weight scale, and though it was heavy in terms of total weight, it felt light in the hands due to its perfect balance.

The lie of Putter #2 is flat and 2 degrees over standard, which translates to 69 degrees, as 71 is the standard lie angle for a putter. The loft is 5 degrees, which is higher than standard, but the club was made this way to allow for the effective loft of the putter being reduced at impact when hitting long putts by employing Hogan's version of the Bobby Locke method. Hogan alternated between a fairly thin and tacky leather grip and a very thick and coarse chord-line grip depending on the course he was scheduled to compete on and whether he figured he would be left with more short and medium-length putts or long ones. This was quite easy to calculate for a man who, on the evening before each tournament round, a couple of hours after practicing putting on the hotel's carpet or hallway, would pull a small blackboard out of his luggage and map out every shot he was going to play—for the entire upcoming round! Where putting was concerned, the thin grip worked better on long putts, when some play and feel in the hands is desirable and distance control is the priority. On short putts, when direction control is the priority, Hogan preferred a thick grip, because it discouraged any manipulation with the hands, and this ensured an on-line stroke and on-line putts.

Putter #2 was so perfectly crafted that the fit boosted Hogan's confidence, as well as providing him with a sense of oneness between the putter and his right hand, right wrist, and right forearm; this was a real bonus, considering this right-sided putting action was critical to controlling all four strokes in his system. Hogan also liked the feel of the ball coming off the putter face with this putter, something he first detected in the 1948 PGA, and which he

attributed to the solid brass putter head.

Hogan believed strongly that his strategy to switch putters would allow him to perform better on the greens and win the game's other major championships. And he was right—stunning the golf world with an incredible comeback performance, highlighted by some superb hole-outs on the greens, winning the 1950 United States Open at Merion Golf Club in Ardmore, Pennsylvania, in a playoff.

Hogan's "fifth round" playoff score of 69, which beat Lloyd Mangrum's 73 and George Fazio's 75, was phenomenal on a day when flagsticks marking the holes were in what controversial golf commentator (and two-time major champion) Johnny Miller calls "sucker pin positions" that required Hogan to pull off all-or-nothing approach shots to hit the ball within birdie range and then, like a true champion, drain the birdie putt. And that Hogan did, more than a couple of times, on his way to his dramatic victory.

Ben Hogan met all the strategic scoring demands at Merion, and in the process proved that the two main strokes in his putting system were working well, as were the two hybrid strokes that are offshoots of each of Hogan's "square" and "inside" main putting strokes. All were made possible by a custom-fit putter and Hogan's never-say-die attitude.

Starting in the Age of Hogan, the 1950s,

and continuing through the Arnold Palmer era of the 1960s and the Nicklaus-Watson era of the 1970s, golf course mowers cut the grass down lower and lower so that, eventually, the putting surfaces looked essentially like they do today, like the green-colored felt tops of billiard tables. But while greens were certainly getting faster by 1950, bent grass greens were still faster overall than Bermuda grass greens, as Ben Hogan discovered and dealt with wonderfully, winning six more majors with Putter #2.

Nevertheless, after adding all these prestigious titles to his trophy case, Hogan, for some inexplicable, seemingly irrational reason, traded his brass putter in for an extremely flat-lie blade putter, with too little loft. As mentioned in Chapter 1, this mind-boggling switcheroo by Hogan cost the Texan a record fifth U.S. Open in 1956.

Sensibly, he switched back to his old faithful brass putter and won the individual Canada Cup title and team trophy that same year, as well as a record fifth Colonial in 1959.

DURING THE 40-year period between 1950 and 1990, the Spalding Cash-In, Spalding T. P. Mills, Wilson Arnold Palmer 8802, Titleist Bull's Eye, Ping Anser, Zebra, and

George Low Wizard (the model that Jack Nicklaus loved so much for a very long time) remained the most popular mass-produced commercial putters.

During this period, Ben Crenshaw won the 1984 Masters wielding a "Little Ben" model and put on such an exhibition at Augusta, sinking putts from all over the greens, that his friend Jack Burke Jr. told him he should put that putter in a glass case, light candles around it, and sell tickets to see it. At least that's the story Jim McLean told me. So it goes to show you what a love affair one can have with a putter. I have known Jim for a long while, and he can tell you stories about the great players and the putters that have worked magic for them, like the White Fang putter that Nicklaus popularized and, for a period in his long career, gave him that can't-miss feeling that every golfer dreams about getting during a round of golf.

Ironically, even today really good pro and amateur putters can be seen putting with one of the aforementioned classics, since they are so well balanced and promote good feel, touch, and distance control, notwithstanding the fact that quite a large number of really good-looking and good-feeling putters, available in golf pro shops, are made right here in the United States.

For what it's worth, I've been putting with the same Spalding T. P. Mills putter for over 25 years, and that's good for confidence, an

HOGAN'S SECRET "DOUBLE-OVERLAP" GRIP

Jules Alexander likely had no idea that he was shooting history at Winged Foot in 1959, when he captured Ben Hogan experimenting while putting on the greens of the club's famous "West Course" and shot the photograph that appears on the cover of this book. I had never seen anyone in the world use this grip before I saw this photograph, let alone Bantam Ben. After examining the photograph, I was able to decipher the positions of the hands when assuming this grip, and then tested it out on my living room carpet with remarkable results. Soon after, I tried the grip out on the putting green at my local course and was amazed how, when employing this grip, you can't help but keep the putter's face dead square to the hole, especially through impact, when coming into the ball with the putter moving low in a streamlined fashion, and putting a pure roll on the golf ball.

What follows is your six-step lesson for gripping the putter with the Hogan "Double-Overlap" grip.

STEP 1:
Take a full-finger or 10-finger baseball grip, with all your fingers on the putter's handle and the thumbs of each hand pointing straight down the grip.

STEP 2:
Turn your right hand clockwise, just a little, until it feels like it is more under than atop the putter's handle, making sure that your right thumb is still pointing pretty much down the shaft, maybe just a little bit off to the side.

STEP 3:
Slide your left hand down the handle so you feel it start to link better to your right hand.

STEP 4:
Move your left forefinger over and somewhat across the third finger of your right hand. Again, refer to Hogan on the cover for visual guidance.

STEP 5:
Push your left hand down, so your hands feel more linked again.

STEP 6:
Slip your right pinky out of its position, turn it under the left forefinger that is draped over the third finger of your right hand, then rest it atop your second finger, in the same way you would rest that pinky over your left forefinger when holding a club with the standard overlap grip.

important key to good putting, according to Ben Hogan and other great players. I like this model on long putts, since it is made the same way Hogan's famous putter was, with the thin flex-point in the shaft providing added feel.

You should pick a putter that's custom-fit to your putting needs, one that possesses a host of attributes, whether it is old or new. What you don't want is a putter, even the newest and most expensive, even one lots of tour pros use, that makes you build a stroke around it rather than swinging a putter that is an extension of what you stand for, literally, at address and also during the start-to-finish action of any one of the four strokes in Ben Hogan's innovative system.

> You should pick a putter that's custom-fit to your putting needs, one that possesses a host of attributes.

Beginning in 1990, a revolution occurred in putter design. Equipment companies started inventing new putters in multiple styles with different club head designs; with inserts in the putter head made of exotic metals, plastic, or rubber; and models featuring varying lies, lofts, weights, grip styles, sweet spot markings, and shaft lengths and types. At the same time, they also became more bullish about putting advertisements.

In turn, this new direction in technology triggered new enthusiasm among amateur golfers, with the average player suddenly becoming interested in learning to putt more proficiently, whereas previously driving was the area of the game that mattered most. Suddenly, golfers wanted to buy a putting game, spending a couple hundred dollars on a putting club that would do all the work, just as they had done in previous years when spending big bucks on a new driver, thinking foolishly that expensive equipment could be a substitute for practice. And with the economy doing well, these fancy newfangled putters flew off the racks at pro shops around the country.

The 9/11 tragedy and the downward plunge of the economy that followed soon after forced golf club manufacturers to stop making new lines of putters. Consequently, golfers started looking instead for someone, somewhere, to provide a tip or new theory to help them putt more proficiently. Golf instructors affiliated with the PGA, golf publications such as *GOLF Magazine, Golf Digest*, and *Golf Tips*, book agents, editors of publishing houses, PGA Tour players moonlighting as writers of instruction books and/or putting how-to articles, and producers at the Golf Channel all became aware of the needs of golfers and jumped on the bandwagon.

Out of the blue, a hodgepodge of way-out putting theories, putting philosophies, and putting methods hit the golf marketplace and were pitched as brand-new, yet actually were old putting tips repackaged. Then the biggest disappointment of all: Tiger Woods's first-ever instructional book, *How I Play Golf* (2001), was published. And though it was well promoted and sold a ton of copies, it failed to deliver the goods on Woods's putting. What's more, although Golf Channel, CBS, NBC, and ABC commentators were notorious for running clips of Tiger sinking long, breaking putts, his ranking in the putting statistics lists, compiled for PGA Tour events and separately for the major championships, was nowhere near as great as in days past.

Today, in 2013, an increasing number of recreational golfers are realizing that wild putting methods such as the claw grip stroke or the split-handed stroke, all of which are euphemistically called unorthodox and previously were so well promoted that they inspired high hopes, are in reality geared to only a very few players and require hours and hours of practice time to learn and maintain—time the average person simply doesn't have. Consequently, avid golfers who play the most rounds and according to various surveys spend the most

money on golf are still waiting for the answer to the question: "How can I become a better putter?"

"There are sundry styles of putting strokes and the number of methods seems to be expanding," says Phil Ritson. "While I don't want to criticize anything that works, I believe that many of the unconventional methods you see contribute more to a player's confidence than to providing any tangible physical advantage. I really don't think there's anything that can beat a solid repeating stroke pattern utilizing a conventional length putter and a tried-and-true reverse overlap putting grip."

I once agreed with Phil. Now I know one repeating stroke is not enough. Why? Hogan proved you need different putting strokes for different length putts and when putting on greens with different type grass, most notably bent or Bermuda grass greens. Furthermore, now that I've tried Ben Hogan's unique putting grip as pictured on the cover of this book—a grip that has never before been brought to light—I will no longer be using the reverse overlap grip that Phil references. Maybe Phil won't either!

I'm confident that if you read and absorb my analysis of Hogan's four-stroke putting system in Chapter 6 and either buy a bespoke putter or work with your local pro to customize your putter, you will have all the tools you'll need to truly improve as a putter.

The secret to success is to stay the course for learning and physically grooving all the putting strokes in Ben Hogan's system, but in addition heeding this warning: A putter that's not custom-fit can be dangerous to your putting game, namely, because it fights your natural, comfortably correct setup and stroke tendencies and, worse, makes you putt a different way, the wrong way, which would surely be a waste after learning Ben Hogan's four-stroke system. In short, a putter that does not fit you properly causes you to develop bad putting habits.

AS YOU go through the putting improvement process, it's also critical that you appreciate that it makes no difference whatsoever if you buy a putter for $1 at a thrift store or spend $500 for a new model, as long as you and your local golf pro agree that the club's features suit your personal setup and stroke positions, such that they are an extension of you when you set up to putt and stroke putts across a green toward the hole, with the full intention of holing out.

I'm optimistic about your putting future for a couple of reasons.

First, I'm told by various golf insiders that 64% of "avid golfers" (those who play more than 72 rounds per year), such as President Barack Obama, would rather be a superb putter than a superb driver, meaning the *GOLF Magazine* survey conducted back when I was at the publication still holds true.

Second, you purchased *Hogan on the Green*.

If you are one of the few golfers lucky enough to be able to putt well with a standard putter off the rack, consider yourself blessed. For the majority of you other golfers, be prepared to spend a few hours, if not a few days, testing various models as you look for the proper fit. Just like when buying a new pair of shoes, finding a good fit takes time and effort. But you'll know immediately when the fit is right. Just understand, a putter is not like leather. It will not stretch and you cannot break it in. So take this shopping expedition seriously and be sure to follow the upcoming guidelines so that you end up with a putter with the perfect customized specifications suited to you and your putting game. I say "you," because such factors as your height, the length of your arms, the size of your hands, and your posture at address all play an important role in determining such elements as the thickness of the putter's grip, the lie and loft of the putter, its length and weight—and all else that goes into a custom fit.

THE SPECIFICATIONS OF A PUTTER: What Hogan Did and What You Need to Consider When Tailored for a Custom-Fit Putter

Grip Type

Putter grips come in a variety of styles, with the paddle grip the most common. The top is flat and easily accommodates the thumbs that most professional golfers, including Ben Hogan and Jack Nicklaus, like to see resting flat and pointing straight down the paddle line. The flat area on Hogan's grip, however, was narrower than others, and this allowed him to position his thumbs correctly in place, with no worries about them falling off track to the sides of the grip, especially after he applied relatively downward pressure.

Grips also come in different materials, with leather and rubber being the most common, plastic and metal the least common. Ben Hogan, at different stages of his career, putted with grips made of leather and a rubber composite. For most of his career, Hogan preferred a leather version of the paddle-type grip, since he liked the feeling of "morphing" his fingers down into the grip, thereby establishing a stronger connection between his hands and the putter. Jack Nicklaus, on the other hand, preferred a round leather grip versus the paddle type, only because of consistency because he had round leather grips of the finest quality were on his other clubs.

Hogan went through stages of experimenting, toiling in his workshop to tweak all his clubs. One result of this overtime work: Hogan put on his favorite putter a new coarse rubber grip with stringy threads running through it, what is known as a chord-grip or chord-line grip. It gave him a feeling of security that there would be no slippage in his hands. The added bonus of this grip was that it was round and matched the handles on his other clubs, yet was much thicker.

Incidentally, even in Hogan's day, maybe 5% of pros, tops, used this chord-grip on their clubs, because of its harshness and because it tended to do a number on the leather glove they wore. Hogan wore a glove, too, but not when putting. Nicklaus, just to make a comparison between two great players, preferred to putt with his glove on, again for reasons of comfort and consistency.

Ben Hogan is the only golf pro I know of who has ever used a round chord-grip on a putter. But he proved he knew what he was doing by making his way to the winner's

Ben Hogan in his at-home club maker's workshop, working on a fairway wood. Most of the time in his shop was spent tweaking the driver, sandwedge, and putter. According to late writer and editor Desmond Tolhurst of *GOLF Magazine,* Ben rarely let anyone see what he was doing to his putter.

circle 63 times during his career. When selecting your own grip, test out various types with the aid of a pro, and select the one that gives you the best feeling and yields the best results on the green.

Grip Size

During his career Hogan switched off between a fairly thin leather grip and a very thick chord-line grip. Your choice of grip thickness has a lot to do with the type of putting stroke you employ. The size of your hands plays a role, too. Should you possess large hands, try a built-up grip. A rubber or chord-line grip is made thicker by blowing off the old grip with an air gun or simply cutting it off. Underneath, wrapped around the putter's shaft, are two types of tape: masking and double-sided. The more layers you add, the thicker the grip.

As a general rule, golfers with small hands need only one wrap of double-sided tape under the putter grip. Golfers with medium-size hands normally go with one double-sided layer and one layer of masking tape. Those of you with large hands, like Hogan, should add two layers of each type of tape. But, again, this is personal. Herbert Warren Wind told me about watching Hogan replace his leather grip with a chord-line grip. Hogan used three layers of each tape, and when Wind looked at the grip, it appeared ready to burst open.

Should you control the stroke with some shoulder action, as Hogan did later in his career, bringing the big muscles into the putting action just a little bit, such that his hands were not in total control of the stroke, then you need a thicker grip.

Should you putt just like Hogan did for most of his career, with the right hand and right wrist playing a vital role on the backstroke and the right forearm pushing the putter through on the down-stroke, then you need a fairly thin grip—of course, depending on the size of your hands—but again, nothing is really cast in bronze. I can only provide guidelines and share with you Ben Hogan's policies, philosophies, and procedures governing grip size choices for his putting club.

Caution: If the grip on your putter is too thick, it will tend to limit greatly your sense of feel or touch, and this hinders distance control. Ben Hogan, as I pointed out, preferred a thick grip, but he always knew when the grip was too thick, and so should you. If the putts you hit fall consistently short of the hole or finish right of the target and short, the grip is too thick. Don't worry, however; your local pro or club maker can fix this problem by removing the grip and removing some tape from underneath, then regripping the putter.

A putter grip that is too thin will encourage loose hand action, causing the putter face to close at impact, with the ball usually hit

The lie of this putter is perfect.

This putter is too upright.

This putter is too flat.

left of the hole and too hard. Or, sensing this is going to happen, just before impact the player grips hard, hinders the putter's release, and blocks the putt out to the right.

Lie

Lie is the angle the shaft of the putter makes with the grass on the green when the putter is sitting on the ground or "soled" in its natural position. This feature of the putter should never be taken for granted, because if the lie is incorrect, say on a new putter you've just purchased, you will be prevented from making your normal putting stroke. You probably won't feel this either, which makes matters worse. The reason is that you'll start changing your stroke to accommodate the lie of the putter. Worse still, once you start missing—and you will miss the hole—you'll change your stroke again, getting rid of all remnants of your original good stroke. This is not how putting equipment works. The putter you use should complement your existing setup and stroke. This dictum translates to putting with a custom putter.

The standard lie angle of a putter is 71 degrees, meaning that if you need a putter that is more upright, say 3 degrees over standard, the putter you play with should boast a lie angle of 74 degrees, the same as Hogan's first putter that he used to win nearly 25

PGA tournaments. Should you feel you need a putter that is flatter because you feel cramped by the upright putter and more comfortable standing farther away, you may want to try a putter with a flat lie angle of 2 degrees over standard, or 69 degrees. As you go down from the standard 71 degrees of lie angle, the angle gets shallower.

The biggest consideration in choosing a putter with the correct lie is how high or low the player positions his or her hands when setting up to putt. Tall players who set their hands high at address require an upright putter, while short players and players of medium height with "low hands" tend to putt better with a putter featuring a flat lie. Ben Hogan fit into the latter category.

If the bottom, or "sole," of the putter sits flush to the ground, with no air or just enough air between the green's surface and the bottom of the putter head's toe such that a dollar bill could just barely be slipped under it, the lie of the putter is perfect for you.

If the toe of the putter is sticking up, with lots of air between the putter and the green, the putter's lie angle is too upright and needs to be flattened in a lie-loft machine.

If the heel of the putter is off the ground, the putter's lie angle is too flat to suit the player's stroke action and thus needs to be made more upright, or replaced, depending on the type of putter and the severity of the problem.

Loft

The standard loft on a putter when delivered from the factory is 3 degrees. Should you employ a level straight back-straight through stroke, à la Ben Hogan on short and medium-length putts, you'll want to swing a putter with around 2 degrees of loft.

Should you employ an inside-square-inside stroke like Hogan preferred to employ on long putts, you should putt with a putter loft of around 5 degrees.

Please appreciate here that, as Hogan proves, different putting situations call for you to employ different techniques, so you have to find a putter with a loft that can accommodate all variations.

Following a long experimental process, Hogan putted with an upright putter with a minimal degree of loft (Putter #1) and won nearly 25 PGA tournaments. However, the putter he used to win all his major championships decided by stroke play featured more loft (Putter #2).

Length

This may surprise you, but a player's height has little to do with being fitted for a putter of the correct length. The distance from your hands to the ground, after you have set up to putt, is the most critical element. Players with short arms or players who like to keep their hands high should use a putter between

36 and 38 inches long. Players with long arms and/or low hands should use a putter about 34 inches long.

In Hogan's early days on tour, he stood up taller at address, with his hands high, and found that a putter 38 inches long worked best. When he felt more comfortable crouching more (yet never stooping) and keeping his hands low, he preferred to use a 36-inch putter.

Shaft Type

The most common types of shafts in putters today are steel and graphite. Touch and feel putters, who depend on the hands and wrists to control the stroke, should select a putter with a medium-flex shaft, since there is some play in this type of shaft that will complement the touch putter. I'd recommend starting with steel first, since graphite can offer too much "play," as Hogan discovered, having tested graphite. He preferred a medium-flex shaft made of steel (Putter #1).

Players who control the putter with their arms and shoulders will generally putt better with a putter featuring a firm shaft, typically one marked S for stiff. Hogan preferred an extra-stiff steel shaft in Putter #2, typically known as an X-Shaft, but only because he started depending a little more on the big muscles of the shoulders to aid the right forearm in the down-stroke push action. Frankly,

though, this was late in his career, some 3 years after he blistered the back nine of Augusta National with that phenomenal score of 30.

Weight

Hogan's first putter weighed out at D-2 on the swing-weight scale. His second putter weighed out at D-5. If you are a laid-back player like Hogan was, with a naturally slow tempo to your stroke, and/or you play most of your golf in the southern United States or the Caribbean where the grass on the greens is coarse (for example, in Florida or Bermuda), you will probably perform better on the greens with a heavy putter.

On the other hand, if you are a Type A personality and swing the putter at a fairly fast but controlled tempo, and you play most of your golf on a course with fast bent grass greens, you will find that a light putter will suit you much better than a heavy one.

Ben Hogan's first putter, Putter #1, was fairly light in terms of dead weight, which is different than swing weight; it is a measurement calculated on a special scale that takes into consideration various sources of weight and their juxtaposition. For example, putting a new thick grip on a putter with a light head will dramatically and negatively influence swing weight, or the overall "weighted balance" of the club.

In terms of the club's balance, the idea is to have one end of the club sort of equal the other, like two people on a seesaw balanced in the air, as opposed to one down on the ground and one high up. This subject can get complex, so just know that, for example, if the head on your putter is light and you add a very thick grip at the other end, you may want to consider adding lead tape to the putter's head to bring the club's weighted balance or swing weight back to a balanced yin-yang state.

Hogan's second putter, Putter #2, featured a heavy solid brass head and a very thick shaft that added even more total weight to the putter. But since both ends were heavy, the putter was in balance.

You definitely need to speak to your pro about this feature of a club, simply because so many variables come into play. But at least now you have the swing-weight "specs" of Ben Hogan's putters to give you some guidance in picking a putter of your own. And that's a good thing, since Hogan had a tremendous knowledge of golf equipment, as did club maker Gene Sheeley, a helpful source of information on club specifications and Hogan's only true mentor on club makeup.

CHAPTER 6
ALL SYSTEMS GO

These tried-and-true principles for setting up and employing all four putting techniques in Ben Hogan's innovative system will help you master the art of hitting short, medium-range, and long on-target putts with maximum distance control.

Ben Hogan knew when he committed to solving the mysteries of putting that he would need to sacrifice time on the course for time on the practice green, working to determine the best setup position from which to employ any of the four strokes in the putting system he was perfecting. Hogan was also fully aware that he needed to spend time testing out different types of putters to find what specifications, relative to such elements as lie angle and degrees of loft, best allowed for a feeling of oneness between his right forearm, wrist, hand, and the putter, and deliver the proper mechanics for all four strokes in his system virtually automatically.

With his patented mind-over-matter determination and an extraordinary degree of meticulousness, Hogan pushed on, studying the putting techniques of great players from the past and present in an attempt to build the model address from which two main putting strokes—a square-to-square upright action and an inside-down the line flatter action—plus one offshoot putting action of the square stroke and one offshoot

Walter Travis had a tremendous influence on Ben Hogan's putting game. Hogan tried and liked the bent-elbows position shown here, as well as the weak left-hand grip position that Travis used when holding the handle of the putter, as this helped the putter head stay on-line while being directed by the right hand, whereas a less square and stable position would not have allowed this to occur during the back and through putting actions.

of the inside stroke, for a total of four strokes, could be employed.

Hogan's breakthrough came when he discovered the ideal setup model to emulate, in the person of Australian Walter Travis. What Hogan liked so much about Travis's setup, which he copied pretty much to the letter after testing it out with much success, was the way Travis let his arms bend freely at the elbows and then kept them closely connected to his body for added security, knowing that in putting, as teacher Phil Ritson says, "the fewer moving parts, the better."

The locked-in position of the arms that Travis established at address promoted a hinging action of the right wrist on the back-stroke and uninterrupted straightening of the right wrist on the down-stroke. In turn, this ensured that the return of the putter into impact would be a perfectly timed, on-path action, making for pure contact between the putter's face and the ball, which is why Hogan modeled his address and wrist action after Travis's, while at the same time adding his own personal nuances to the putting setup and start-to-finish stroke.

The characteristic super-narrow Walter Travis stance, with both feet pointed outward and the heels nearly touching, did not suit Hogan, since it failed to provide him a sense of stability. Hogan had tested various stances and preferred positioning the feet down, spread practically shoulder-width

This view of Ben Hogan's reverse overlap grip shows the weak left hand position that Hogan used on all putts. It also shows the strong, turned-under position of the right hand. Both of these positions were triggered by Hogan studying the setup of Walter Travis.

apart. An overly narrow stance, Hogan learned through experimentation, can cause you to pick the putter up too abruptly on the back-stroke and chop down on the ball.

Whereas Travis balanced his weight evenly between his two feet, Hogan placed as much as 70% of his body weight on his left foot, calling this his "tripod position" for setting up. By leaning most of his weight left, thereby stabilizing his body, Hogan prevented any swaying off the ball on the back-stroke, which would cause him to swing the putter back on too rounded a path and employ too long an action, a fault that would throw off the timing of the putting stroke and, ultimately, lead to off-line putts hit much too hard.

As for Travis's ball position, playing the ball forward in the stance worked best for Hogan as well, as did doing exactly what Travis did on short putts: setting the eyes behind the ball and directly over the target line.

Hogan also modeled his weak left-hand grip position after Travis, finding that this hold, more than a strong or neutral left-hand grip, was best for short and medium-range putts, since it makes it easier to keep the putter's face square to the hole and employ a straight-back straight-through putting stroke.

As much as Hogan liked Travis's setup, he did not copy the Australian amateur's short left thumb position. Hogan outstretched the thumb atop the grip and straight down the shaft, a position he obviously believed gave him a stronger sense of security, since he was so against any gaps between grip and hand that could lead to slippage. On short and medium-length putts, when you want to keep the putter moving along the target line going back and coming through, it's easier to execute this movement using a "long thumb" rather than a "short thumb" position.

While we are reviewing the grip, which some teachers call the "engine room" of the

The photograph (above) shows Ben Hogan's grip for hitting long putts.

putting setup, let's review some other vital aspects as each applies to the new system Hogan developed.

First, you will find that by holding the club with a grip pressure of around 7 on a scale of 1 to 10, as Ben Hogan did, you will have good control of the putter and ensure that you return the club squarely to the ball at impact.

On long putts, you should follow Hogan's example, too. Long putts require a different strategy. Touch is most critical, so you'll want to hold the handle of the putter with a pres-

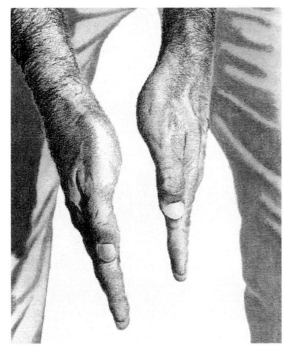

A high percentage of great putters from the past and present grip the club with hands in this palms-parallel position.

Hogan gripped the club to hit a short, medium-length, or long putt, he made sure that the palms of both hands were in the position shown in the accompanying illustration.

While Hogan was a chameleon of sorts, in that he constantly changed his setup and stroke from tournament to tournament depending on the type of greens he was competing on, he did still always rely on a set of principles that he applied to each specific situation he confronted on the greens.

PRINCIPLE #1: When hitting short putts on slow greens, and you prefer to use a more lofted putter than standard, set up with your left hand just a little bit in front of the golf ball, and mirror this position through impact to effectively reduce the loft of the putter and virtually guarantee a pure, slightly faster rolling end-over-end ball that will counteract the slow-rolling green.

PRINCIPLE #2: When hitting long putts on super-fast greens, and you prefer to use a putter with less loft than what is built into the face of a standard off-the-rack putter, set your hands slightly behind the ball. This starting position will allow you to keep the putter moving low to the green's surface and add a slight degree of loft to the putter at impact, so the ball will roll a little slower on the slick green

sure of 6. Hogan found that holding the club with the same reverse overlap grip on long putts that he used for short and medium-length putts (but letting his left forefinger drape over the first three fingers of his right hand, instead of only the right pinky) promoted the proper amount of wrist action and allowed him to put the right amount of "oomph" into the stroke.

Whichever grip you choose to play with, another vital element of the Hogan system involves the palms of both hands. When

when struck a little outside the sweet spot and closer to the toe of the club.

PRINCIPLE #3: Set up with your right foot perpendicular to the target line on medium-length putts; this position will help you swing the putter straight back and straight through along the target line. This adjustment works great, as Ben Hogan proved, on greens covered in poa annua grass common on the West Coast of the United States, especially if the ball is struck dead center in the sweet spot of the putter face that is almost always right under the neck of the club.

PRINCIPLE #4: Set up on long putts with your right foot fanned out slightly about 25 degrees, as this will promote the inside-down the line putting stroke so vital to hitting long putts on slow greens.

PRINCIPLE #5: On medium-length putts on very slow greens, set your eyes just slightly inside the target line, as this one small adjustment will allow you to swing the putter on the slightest inside-to-inside path and impart just a little bit of sidespin on the ball at impact. This will be all that's needed to hit a firm on-line putt without changing the tempo of your stroke or lengthening your action.

PRINCIPLE #6: On long putts hit over slow Bermuda greens, set your eyes a few inches inside the target line, yet no farther back as the putt distance lengthens. This inside position will promote the desired inside path and slightly curved arc of stroke needed for hitting long putts like Ben Hogan, who learned this technique by observing Bobby Locke; Locke completed the stroke by letting the toe of the club lead its heel through the impact zone and impart a touch of hook-spin on the ball. (Be careful not to exaggerate this setup position or the putter will move along an exaggerated in-to-out path, causing the ball to be pushed right of the hole.)

In the same way that Ben Hogan realized that his power-fade would not work on all courses all of the time and that he had to be able to match a particular shot to a particular course situation, golfers like you must face the reality that to shoot the lowest possible scores it is necessary to match a specific on-course putting situation with one of the following four techniques. This logical approach to putting, in which a specific stroke is matched to a particular length putt and/or putting surface, will benefit any golfer looking for real answers to the putting problems that have plagued them. The actions that Hogan used interchangeably during a single round of golf, depending on the putting situation he faced, are as follows:

A square-to-square putting action for short and medium-length putts on fast rolling bent grass greens;

An inside-square-down the line putting stroke for long putts on fast bent grass greens;

A hybrid form of the square stroke, involving a top-of-the-ball hit for short and medium-length putts on Bermuda grass greens; and

A hybrid form of the inside stroke, requiring the player to impart a slight degree of right-to-left sidespin on the ball when hitting long putts on slow Bermuda grass greens.

FAULTS AND FIXES

Here is what you can learn from the common putting mistakes of golf's greatest players, with simple instructions for correcting your mistakes.

Fault

Even the great Arnold Palmer found out that gripping the club with a "death grip" and bringing the right shoulder into the putting stroke can distort the feel for the putter head and play havoc with distance control. During his heyday, Palmer performed famously on both fast greens (such as at Augusta National and Cherry Hills, where he captured his only U.S. Open title in 1960) and slow greens (such as at British Open venues

One error that Arnold Palmer seemed to make whenever he was in contention at the PGA Championship was to grasp the club too tightly on short putts, with a pressure of 10 on a 1–10 scale. Worse, while cutting off feel for the putter head, Palmer looked to his right shoulder muscles to provide the "oomph" behind the stroke, and this is why you see it jut out here slightly, moving in front of the left shoulder. He got that all right—and then some, hitting the ball so hard that it rolled several feet past the hole.

The Hogan Fix

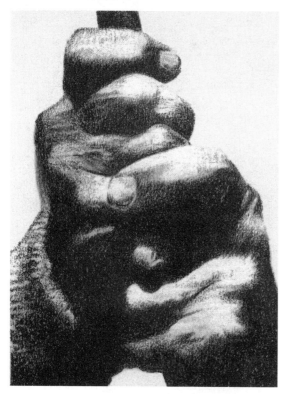

Should you share the same problem that Arnold Palmer sometimes experienced, try changing to the standard reverse overlap grip, where the right forefinger rests atop the right pinky, as shown here, and hold the club much more lightly. This will enhance your feel for the putter, make for a freer stroke, and help you hit the ball the proper distance without ever having to bring the shoulder farthest from the ball into play.

Troon and Royal Birkdale, links courses where he won in 1961 and 1962). But when it came time to compete in the last major championship of the year, the PGA in August—the only major championship that Palmer failed to win—at venues that boasted medium-speed greens, he struggled, strangely, on putts from 20 feet out.

Whether the added pressure of trying to win that elusive PGA had something to do with Palmer knocking makeable putts from the 20-foot range well past the hole, I don't know. What I do know is that what Palmer did when hitting those types of putts would not fit into Hogan's system of putting.

Palmer's mistake was that in trying so hard to keep the putter head moving straight down the target line with its face square to the hole, he squeezed the heck out of the grip with those huge hands of his. In doing this, he cut off all feel for the putter and brought the real killer into the stroke—the right shoulder, hoping, I guess (perhaps subconsciously), that the big muscles of the right shoulder would help give the ball a little extra "oomph" and get it to the hole.

Fault

Ben Crenshaw's misdirected long putts on slow greens can be traced to a stance problem. Throughout his career, Crenshaw putted superbly, with many golf experts saying he

Ben Crenshaw's open stance caused him problems when hitting long putts on slow greens.

was the best putter of all time. Still, on courses featuring slow greens, which are a touch putter's worst nightmare, Crenshaw did not perform nearly as well. Confronting such a situation, as Crenshaw did several times on British Open courses where the greens just do not roll the same way as they do on bent grass greens in America, he often misdirected long putts.

Crenshaw played out of the same open stance he used on short putts, with the left foot dropped back several inches from the target line. On the back-stroke he swung the putter along an inside path, and that's fine so far. However, on the down-stroke, in trying to counter the slow green, he swung his putter at a faster speed and thus followed the path of his open feet, thereby causing him to pull the ball left of the hole.

The Hogan Fix

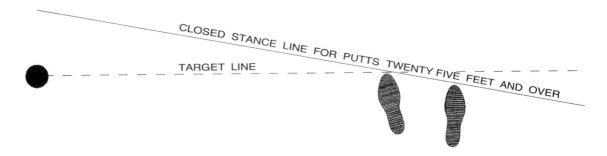

When faced with a long putt, play out of a closed stance, but one with the right foot dropped back from the left just a few inches, not one so exaggerated as Bobby Locke's. Even Ben Hogan did not go to that extreme. Never stand open like Ben Crenshaw.

Seve Ballesteros's incorrect and mistimed hand and wrist action caused the face of the putter to come into impact open—pointing right of the hole—and that is exactly where the ball finished.

Fault

Twice a winner of the Masters (1980 and 1983) and a three-time winner of The Open Championship (1979, 1984, and 1988), Seve Ballesteros relied on great eye-hand coordination to sink putts on fast greens, like those at Augusta National, and on slower greens, likc those on England's Royal Lytham links. But putting on grainy poa annua greens, like those commonly found on the West Coast of the United States, drove the Spaniard crazy. And this can be traced to mistimed wrist action on the down-stroke.

When putting on these types of greens, Seve would sometimes try to help the ball along, to get it moving faster by increasing the tempo of his stroke. Worse, Seve sometimes let his left wrist hinge back, thereby causing his right hand to turn under the left in the hitting area and the putter's face to open or point right of the target at impact. The result: a putt pushed to the right of the hole.

The Hogan Fix

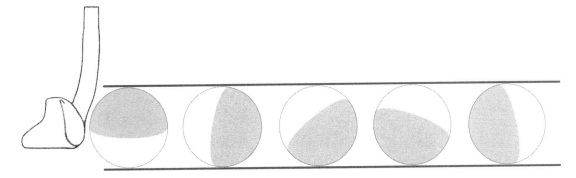

Maintain the same tempo of stroke you would use normally for the same length putt. Don't even think about your hands and wrists. The countermeasure you should use when putting on greens with heavy grain is to contact the top half of the ball, as this will get the ball rolling nicely end over end as soon as it is struck. When you follow this example, set by Ben Hogan, you increase your hole-out percentages. Through impact, the back of the left hand should stay square to the target line, with the left wrist firm. The right wrist should straighten and follow.

There were a lot of qualities of Sam Snead's stroke that coincided with Ben Hogan's putting philosophy. But Snead tended to make one glaring setup error and another error during the back-stroke that hindered his delivery of the putter into the ball and thus hindered the end result. Sam took much too wide a stance, and although he swung the club on the desired inside path for hitting long putts on slow greens, the putter rose too high into the air at the top of the back-stroke. When you do this, you have to do a lot of manipulating with your hands on the down-stroke to prevent the club coming into impact too late, as the putter is swinging up.

Fault

Sam Snead, winner of three PGAs, three Masters, and a British Open, failed to ever win a United States Open championship. The mistake that Snead made on long putts on fast greens, the super-fast surfaces common to all U.S. Open venues, can be traced to a faulty stance width and back-stroke. Snead swung the putter back correctly on an inside path in the takeaway, just as Ben Hogan did. But, ultimately, the Virginian employed too long a back-stroke, owing to too wide a stance, with the club rising too high off the ground. Consequently, he'd match the arc coming down, such that the putter face started leveling off at the start of the down-stroke and then moved up sharply at the moment of impact, causing the ball to slide and skid and bobble at the point of takeoff and finish well short of the hole.

The Hogan Fix

Should you be hitting bad long putts on slow greens in a similar fashion to Sam Snead, try standing open your both feet a few inches less than shoulder-width apart and your right foot closer to the target line than your left foot; this stance will encourage you to employ a shorter, more streamlined, back-stroke. That's the beauty of Hogan's method for hitting these types of putts. You don't need to make an extra-long backswing or to swing extra-hard. The ball will reach the hole if you just follow Hogan's example of coming into impact with the toe of the club leading the heel and imparting a little hook-spin on the ball, à la Bobby Locke, whose technique Hogan emulated—with one caveat: Swing at a fairly slow 1-2 tempo.

HOGAN'S SHORT/MEDIUM PUTTING TECHNIQUES

Just on the basis of how Ben Hogan started his putting stroke—putting the club in motion—he was considered a rebel by those who had been brainwashed into believing golf was a left-sided game. Tommy Armour, the Silver Scot, had tried to convince the so-called golf experts years earlier that controlling the entire action of the backswing by pulling the club gently back with the right hand was more natural. All Ben Hogan did was apply this thinking to putting, and it works wonders, especially when you also allow your right wrist to hinge practically at the same time you begin gently pulling the putter back straight along the target line. This is, of course, far easier to do if you set your shoulders square to the putting line, as Hogan did.

Two commonalities when hitting short and medium-length putts on either bent grass or Bermuda grass greens are that you position your eyes directly over the target line, just behind the ball (above, left) and keep the club moving down the target line on the through-swing (above, right).

Ben Hogan found that the most natural way to putt was to gently pull on the handle of the club and hinge the right wrist on the back-stroke (above, left) and to push the club gently through while straightening the right wrist on the down-stroke (above, right).

The down-stroke action that Hogan employed was controlled by a push action of the right forearm and palm. As you begin this pushing action, the right wrist must now start straightening, practically simultaneously, opposite to the actions of the back-stroke. Keeping your head and body dead-still such that the smooth rhythmic action of the stroke is maintained allows the putter head to swing back straight along the target line, square to the hole. (On breaking putts that curve, the putter face will be square to the aiming point to one side of the hole, depending on whether the ball is going to curve left or right, a target you should have picked out during your prestroke routine.)

Despite going against every tenet prescribed by those golf instructors who call golf a "game of opposites"—meaning that right-handed putters should control the stroke with the left side, not the right side—this right-hand controlled backswing and right forearm/right palm/right wrist–controlled down-stroke action is by far the easier method of putting to learn and to put into practice on the course.

It was not until much later that pros such as Jack Nicklaus and Billy Casper were smart enough to pick up on Ben Hogan's system of putting, but Hogan let on that he didn't know. The reason is, according to Herbert Warren Wind, that Hogan told him that Billy and Jack (and, in some respects, Arnold Palmer) were "guinea pigs." Hogan was interested in seeing how they did using his techniques, with their own small nuances added to personalize their strokes and make them their own. When all three succeeded with flying colors, Hogan knew his system would likely work for all golfers.

For Performing Your Best on Fast-Rolling Bent Grass Greens

Rather than employing either the commonly recommended straight back-straight-through method or the inside-square-inside action or, alternatively, one of the more unorthodox methods of putting, such as the cross-handed or split-handed stroke, Ben Hogan employed a square stroke for hitting short putts on bent grass greens.

In hitting medium-range putts on the same fast-rolling surface, Hogan kept the length of stroke the same as for short putts and simply increased the tempo of the overall action, but only slightly. He maintained a smooth rhythm, a key to coordinating the movement of the hands and arms with the movement of the putter in a synchronized manner.

As to the path of the putter, obviously you'd like to keep it moving along the target line you've chosen for as much of the stroke as possible. The reason is that staying on this path can only make the roll of the putt more consistent than if you swing the putter on an exaggerated inside path. To do this, though, you need a putter featuring a straight up and down shaft that forms a 90-degree angle with the head of the putter and that's built like a croquet mallet—which is technically out of the question and illegal to boot, according to the rules of golf. Furthermore, you'd have to manipulate the club artificially to the top of the back-stroke, and with this tense start, the likelihood of hitting a good putt is slim.

The golfer's best security against hitting a bad putt is to make a natural stroke of the putter like Hogan, controlling the back and through motions of the putter by moving as few parts as possible; in Hogan's case, what's essential is concentrating on the hinging and straightening action of the right wrist and keeping the putter's face square to the path of the stroke. If the putter face remains square to this path throughout the entire back-stroke and down-stroke, this means it will automatically be square to the target at impact.

For Mastering Slow-Rolling Bermuda Grass Greens

When hitting both short and medium-length putts on slower greens, Ben Hogan employed what top teacher Jim Hardy calls a hybrid stroke. To employ this method of Hogan's, position the ball forward, opposite the left instep; this will allow you to contact the ball a fraction later in the stroke, with the putter's face positioned to make contact with the middle portion of the ball rather than its bottom portion.

In observing Ben Hogan putting on film, I could see that he believed this a very useful setup adjustment. It allowed him (and will enable you) to get the ball rolling with overspin as quickly as possible—in fact, the split second it is struck. The faster you can get the ball rolling with overspin, the more truly the ball will roll, particularly on this

type of coarse putting surface. If you hit down really sharply on the ball when putting on Bermuda grass greens, the ball will inevitably hop and often get thrown off-line right at the start. So I advise you to set up with the ball a little more forward in your stance and your hands even with the ball, which is something Tiger Woods did back in 2000 when he putted his best en route to winning three major championships.

One of the keys to hitting solid putts like this one hit by Ben Hogan in the Canada Cup of 1956 is contacting the top half of the golf ball rather than its lower portion.

HOGAN'S LONG-PUTT TECHNIQUES

Even when hitting a long uphill putt, Ben Hogan still played the percentages, concentrating on rolling the ball at a speed that allowed the ball to "die" in the hole.

Asking the caddie to attend the flagstick, as he is doing here for Ben Hogan, helped Hogan and will help you focus on a clear target and, as a result, be a better judge of distance on the green.

Before providing you with the details of this unique long-range putting stroke, I want to give credit where credit is due and tell you that it was Claude Harmon, Ben Hogan's friend and golf partner, who helped Hogan putt better from long distance by persuading him to stop charging long putts and become a "die putter." The reason for Hogan's improvement is that the hole is essentially bigger to a die putter. If you hit the putt at a slower rate, so that the ball will die into the

hole (rather than at a rate fast enough to land the ball 17 inches past an imaginary hole, as Dave Pelz recommends golfers do), it still has a very good chance of dropping into one of the cup's "side doors" or even the "back door" if it is a little bit off-line.

World Golf Hall of Famer Harry Cooper had observed Hogan practicing putting sometime in the early 1950s and noticed that the length of time he stood still over the ball was increasing and that the pace of his back-stroke was extra-slow while the pace of his down-stroke was faster than normal. So he told Hogan to stop putting in his head and to just set up to the ball as he'd practiced over and over, look at the hole, set the club with the early wrist hinge he preferred, and start the stroke. Hogan took the advice and went on to sink more putts than ever. Of course, Hogan or any other golfer only reaches this cruise-control stage after having learned a fundamentally sound putting stroke through diligent practice. The total putting action becomes ingrained into the muscle memory, and the stroke, triggered in Hogan's case by a gentle pull of the putter with the right hand and simultaneous hinge of the right wrist, operates essentially on automatic pilot.

When the subconscious rather than the conscious mind controls the stroke, you can concentrate on the target and trust the body to swing the putter back, return the putter to a square impact position, and swing the putter through the ball, toward the hole.

One sure way to get you focused more on the target—the $4\frac{1}{4}$-inch-round cup—particularly when facing a long pressure putt in a tournament or weekend match at your country club, when the last thing you want to do is start trying to piece together stroke techniques in your head, is to ask your caddie to attend the flagstick.

Hogan had the caddie do this on long putts to boost confidence, heighten concentration, and relax over the ball. Most important though, it helped him better control distance, since knowing for sure where the hole is and being reminded of its position by having the caddie standing to the side of the hole attending the flagstick helps your depth perception. This strategy is useful whether you are in a situation where you must sink the putt to stay in the game, or when your goal is just to "lag" the ball within an imaginary 2-foot circle surrounding the hole in order to ensure a two-putt green and move on to the next hole. What's more, having the flag attended is a real plus factor when playing during the summer, when glare can hinder your sight and thus make it more difficult to judge distance.

Up until 1956, you could play in a tournament and keep the flagstick in the hole while you were putting on the green, whereas now it has to be removed or attended and then removed by the caddie. So Hogan got used to seeing the flag in the hole. This was one reason why, after the rule changed, he would even have the caddie sometimes attend the flag on medium-length putts, too, in the 10- to 25-foot range, just to feel more secure about the target. Ted Longworth, once the head golf professional at the Glen Garden Club, was the first to suggest Hogan do this, to help his depth perception and distance control.

Whereas some tour professionals are being swayed into adopting a stroke with a path that moves dramatically from inside to inside, when putting on bent grass greens, like those at Augusta National, this is a bad idea. Instead, do what Ben Hogan does here (above) when hitting a long putt on the super-fast greens of Augusta: He completes the stroke by swinging the putter straight down the target line, rather than rotating the club back to the inside, which you cannot get away with on fast bent grass greens. What you don't see is what part of the putter's face contacted the ball. Because this putt was fast to start with due to the slick surface, and it was made faster because Hogan was putting downhill, he contacted the ball closer to the toe end than the heel end of the putter head, rather than the sweet spot located below the neck of the putter's face, in order to "deaden" the hit.

For Performing Your Best on Fast Bent Grass Greens

In hitting long putts, Ben Hogan simplified the action by executing the stroke essentially with just one hand. Those who play the game right-handed, as natural left-handed player Ben Hogan did, should supply the energy for the putting stroke with their right hand, right arm, and right shoulder, while the left hand goes along for the ride, as Hogan's does.

Watching film of Hogan putting, I could see him gently pull the handle of the putter back and push it through, using a one-piece piston-like motion. It's this right-side action that Jack Nicklaus adopted, owing to what he learned from teacher Jack Burke Jr. Nicklaus tweaked this element of the stroke to fit his natural tendencies, though. Nicklaus's method worked far better on short putts than on long putts. The reason is that on putts of over 25 feet, Nicklaus guarded against the putter face swinging inside on the backstroke by grasping the putter's handle firmly with what's called a one-knuckle super-weak grip; he also kept his shoulders square to the target line or slightly open, but never closed (pointing right of target).

In contrast, Hogan gripped the putter lightly to promote feel and touch and distance control. He also allowed his right shoulder to turn clockwise on the backstroke to let the putter swing inside the target line, yet only slightly, with the putter face staying square to the path of the stroke. Furthermore, Hogan turned his right shoulder in a counterclockwise direction on the through-stroke, such that it worked its way back to a position square to the target line. More important, Hogan's natural-feeling right-hand control allowed the putter's face to return to a square impact position, yet with the effective loft of Hogan's 2-degree putter reduced and, in turn, this slightly shut club face position allowing the ball to start rolling immediately and smoothly along the grass. This smooth roll ensures a purer roll of the ball, in terms of both direction and speed.

Whereas speed in the Hogan stroke is controlled by reducing the putter's effective loft at impact, Nicklaus simply swung the putter more briskly—never really fast—which is far harder to gauge on long putts. This is why as great a player as Nicklaus was during his heyday, he was not known as a great long-range putter, as opposed to Tom Watson, his chief rival, who holed many super-long putts, especially en route to winning The Open Championship five times.

Here we see Ben Hogan putting on one of the slow greens of Carnoustie, in Scotland, site of The Open Championship (British Open) in 1953. Hogan putted so brilliantly on this unfamiliar surface, especially from long range, that he won the championship.

For Mastering Slow-Rolling Bermuda Grass Greens

When hitting long putts in the 25- to 75-foot range on very slow-rolling putting surfaces using the Ben Hogan method, allow your left forearm to turn clockwise ever so slightly as your right wrist hinges back, such that the putter head swings open on the back-stroke. On the down-stroke, allow your left forearm to rotate counterclockwise—slowly—while your right wrist straightens, practically simultaneously, so that your right forearm follows counterclockwise extra-slowly, such that the putter's head swings into a closed position, with the toe leading its heel-through impact.

The process of the putter's face opening during the first half of the stroke and closing during the second half of the stroke operates much like a door opening and closing, a visual metaphor to help golfers like you clearly picture and understand Hogan's

stroke mechanics. Still, this stroke takes some practice and should only be tried when you are out playing for fun and not in competition until you have practiced it over and over again. It even took some getting used to for Ben Hogan.

It's the down-stroke action, which imparts the spin on the ball, that makes all the difference to the roll of the ball on slow greens. This happens a split second before the putter's face is about to strike the ball. At this point, Hogan rotates his right forearm over his leading left hand, so that at the moment of impact the putter face shuts slightly. Because of Hogan's unique release action and the shut-face hit of club to ball, a small degree of hook-spin is imparted on the ball at impact, making it roll "hot" at a much faster speed toward the hole, which counteracts the slow Bermuda grass putting surface. More important, this impact action allows the ball to hit the ground and start rolling right away, rather than hopping into the air, with the ball practically guaranteed to roll the desired distance and never come up short.

ACKNOWLEDGMENTS

Writing *Hogan on the Green* and seeing the finished product, with words and pictures relaying, for the first time ever, the important instructional messages tied to the innovative four putting strokes in the shot-making repertoire of legendary golfer Ben Hogan, is very satisfying indeed.

The reason I'm so excited by the publication of *Hogan on the Green* is that it represents a golfer's guidebook for learning how to employ the somewhat unorthodox, yet fundamentally sound and highly functional putting techniques Ben Hogan devised and developed, over years and years, through trial-and-error experimental practice and studying the game's greatest putters from past and present.

Another reason I'm pleased is that *Hogan on the Green* is also a biographical homage, in that it explores Ben Hogan the man and the evolution of the putting methods he mastered.

Frankly, this book could never have come to fruition, and gone from the proposal stage to the publication stage, had it lacked the strong support and vision of Mark Weinstein, the editorially savvy executive editor of Rodale Books.

Fortunately, Deborah Atkinson, my better half of 25 years, convinced me to take a hiatus from working on another book about my discovery of a lost painting by a famous 17th-century Spanish artist I'd been writing for 3 years, which was no easy task. Everyone, at least once in their life, thinks about writing a book, yet only a tiny percentage of individuals ever sit down and actually put pen to paper or, in my case, lots of pencils to lots of yellow legal pads, before beginning to even type a word on what was formerly a typewriter, when I wrote my first book around 25 years ago, and now, thankfully, is a laptop computer that makes the entire process easier—but never easy. As poet William Butler Yeats once said: "I would rather scrub floors than write."

Hogan on the Green was originally sparked by a conversation I had with golf writer John Stobbs, an Englishman with whom, in 1980, I traveled on business to the Isle of Man in a prop plane and discussed Ben Hogan's putting prowess while flying to our destination.

The idea for *Hogan on the Green* went dormant for nearly a decade, and then again for over two decades, for all kinds of reasons. Although the entire backstory is yet to be told, let me just say that one problem had always been the lack of "period" photographs showing Ben Hogan putting.

Thankfully, when the book was resurrected one final time, over a year ago, Getty Images had organized the most complete library of photographs, including rare photos showing Ben Hogan putting during the 1940s and 1950s, that I did not even know existed. These photos really helped me relay the instructional messages on putting and, at the same time, added credibility to *Hogan on the Green*. Thank you to Brian Blankenburg and the team at Getty Images, including all the Getty-affiliated photographers whose work helped this book come to life: Walter Iooss Jr., John Zimmerman, John D. Hanlon, and Don Uhrbrock (*Sports Illustrated*); Joseph Scherschel, Ralph Crane, Robert W. Kelley, Martha Holmes, Carl Mydans, Peter Stackpole, Hans Knopf, A.Y. Owen, and Dean Loomis (Time & Life Pictures); and Bob Thomas (Bob Thomas Sports Photography).

I'm also grateful to the *Evening Standard* in England and the Hulton Archive, and the Augusta National Archive for their "Masters History Images."

Thanks to the Associated Press for a picture showing Ben Hogan and Byron Nelson on the putting green of the Glen Garden Club in Fort Worth, Texas.

Speaking further about the subject of photography, I'm lost for adjectives when describing the work, in black and white, of Jules Alexander, a true professional who I call a "photo artist" because of the wonderful work he creates with a camera. Jules does not take pictures. Jules makes pictures, and he made a great one in 1959 when shooting Ben Hogan putting at Winged Foot Golf Club; this was a shot showing Ben Hogan's "lost grip," which I'd heard whispers of for years but never had seen proof of. Thank you, Jules, for our long professional relationship and, after a lengthy hiatus, for coming up with the best cover shot possible.

The professional expertise and personal recollections of many different people contributed to the material in *Hogan on the Green*, and I am extremely grateful for their time and their insights into Ben Hogan:

Dave Pelz, who I had worked with several times on articles for *GOLF Magazine* and who, to me, is the most knowledgeable coach there is when it comes to the short game and putting.

While Ben Hogan's comments on putting technique are certainly precious, conversations with Hogan's collaborator on *Five Lessons*, Herbert Warren Wind, went a long way toward clearing up questions of chronology regarding the evolution of Hogan's unique putting system, as well as explaining the ins and outs of particular stroke techniques so insightfully. It was evident he studied golf's "ground game" under the best of teachers. Thank you, gentlemen.

When it comes to relaying the instructional messages in the text, I was privileged to have the assistance of three artists: Ron Ramsey, Shu Kuga, and Allen Welkis.

Ron I know from working with him formerly at *GOLF Magazine*, when he was art director for as long as I was senior instruction editor. Ron is actually an artist in his own right, and a great one, too, who possesses the pedigree I was looking for on this project, having done a portrait for Ben Hogan that once hung in the champion's Texas home. Norman Rockwell, whose work graced the covers of the *Saturday Evening Post*, where Ron had worked before coming to *GOLF Magazine*, would have been proud of Ron's work in *Hogan on the Green*, particularly the drawing he did of Hogan that accompanies my introduction.

Shu, a Japan-based artist, has done great work for me in the past for books and magazine articles, so I am happy he was able to make a contribution to *Hogan on the Green*.

Allen fits into the same mold, having illustrated the very successful book *The Tiger Woods Way*, which I wrote in 1997, as well as other titles.

I'm also truly indebted to my dear friend Greg Hood, Ben Hogan's former personal assistant, who provided me with inside information on Hogan, vis-à-vis this great player's putting techniques, personality traits, putting equipment, competitive nature, and love of the oil business.

A belated thank-you to Lesley Jane Fox, a previous mentor of mine, for always believing in me since the late 1970s, when I broke into the golf business by writing humorous short stories on golf, all with a love twist, and golf features and course history profiles, in the family home in Walton-on-Thames, England, and the family villa in Marbella, Spain. You really deserved credit sooner than this for my success.

Last, but certainly not least, I'd be remiss if I neglected to show my gratitude to the Shell Oil Company for the video it produced showing the classic Ben Hogan versus Sam Snead match that took place at the Houston Country Club in May 1964, and aired on television February 21, 1965. Viewing this match once again brought back memories and also offered me great insights into Ben Hogan's putting techniques. Every golfer should own a copy of this tape. Seeing Hogan shoot the winning score of 69 to beat his old rival Snead offers you the best of both worlds, since while you are studying Hogan's putting stroke and comparing it to Sam's, you will be entertained at the same time.

PHOTO AND ILLUSTRATION CREDITS

Photos:

Getty Images: Pages xviii, 2, 3, 5, 28, 32, 43, 60, 63, 68, 70, 71, 74, 76, 77, 78 80, 81, 85, 88, 100, 106, 110, 120, 123, 124, 125, 127, and 129

Associated Press: Page 50

Dave Hanko Photography: Page 135

Illustrations:

Ron Ramsey © 2012: Pages x, 36, 41, 47, 82, 102, 109, 111, 113, 115, 117, 118, and 119

Shu Kuga © 2012: Pages 41, 45, 54, 55, 56, 86, 87, 115, and 116

Allen Welkis © 2012: Pages 108 and 121

Special Insert:

Getty Images: Pages 2, 5, 6, 7, 9, 12, 13, 14, 15, and 16

Ron Ramsey © 2012: Page 3 (top)

Allen Welkis © 2012: Pages 3 (bottom) and 10

ABOUT THE AUTHOR

John Andrisani is the former senior editor of instruction at *GOLF Magazine* and the author or coauthor of more than 30 books on golf, including *The Tiger Woods Way, Think Like Tiger,* and others under his byline, as well as collaborations with the game's greatest players, most notably *Natural Golf,* a one-time Book-of-the-Month Club selection, with the late Seve Ballesteros.

Andrisani is also the coauthor of best-selling books with top-ranked teachers, including *The Plane Truth for Golfers* with Jim Hardy, *The X-Factor Swing* with Jim McLean, and *The Four Cornerstones of Winning Golf* with Butch Harmon.

A former golf instructor and now a two-handicap amateur golfer, and past winner of the World Golf Writers' Championship, Andrisani resides in Florida.

INDEX

Boldface page references indicate photographs and illustrations. An * indicates a photograph or text in the *Special Insert* pages.